memos for managers

Books by Auren Uris

ACTION GUIDE FOR JOB SEEKERS
MASTERY OF MANAGEMENT
THE EXECUTIVE DESKBOOK
THE TURNED-ON EXECUTIVE
THE FRUSTRATED TITAN
THANK GOD IT'S MONDAY
MEMOS FOR MANAGERS

Humor

HOW TO WIN YOUR BOSS'S LOVE,
APPROVAL AND JOB (with coauthor)

memos
for
managers

Auren Uris

Thomas Y. Crowell Company
Established 1834   New York

54157

Acknowledgment is made to The Viking Press, Inc., for permission to quote excerpts from *Memo From David O. Selznick,* selected and edited by Rudy Behlmer, copyright © 1972 by Selznick Properties, Ltd.

Library of Congress Cataloging in Publication Data

Uris, Auren.
  Memos for managers.

  1. Memorandums. I. Title.
HF5719.U75 1975   658.4′53
74–14650
ISBN 0–690–00648–9

1 2 3 4 5 6 7 8 9 10

Acknowledgments

Executives, secretaries, rank-and-file employees, middle managers—people in every organizational echelon who write and read memos—helped write this book. And their experience covers a broad cross-section of business, industry, government, and non-profit service organizations.

Where friends, colleagues, and part-time collaborators have felt free to be identified with the sample memos and other related material they have provided, they have been credited with their contributions. However, many of the communications are personal in nature and anonymity has been requested. Of course, the author has readily agreed and further disguised sources by changes of names and other identifiable elements.

In addition to those people whose contributions have been acknowledged in the text itself, thanks are due to:

These colleagues at the Research Institute of America: Charles Antin, Grace Barrett, Rick Blake, Jane G. Bensahel, Theodore W. Case, Raymond Concannon, Patricia Durston, Robert Herzog, Mary Jollon, Elizabeth Lonahan, Domenica Mortati, Tom Quick, Louise Trenta, and Barbara Whitmore.

For library services and guidance: Mary McKenna Summers and Inese Rudzitis, of the Research Institute library, and Roberta J. Gardner, head librarian of the Dun & Bradstreet Library.

For outstanding help with the physical preparation of the manuscript: Winifred Mathie, Beth Harding, Ellen Taylor, and Fay Rossi.

Doris Horvath assisted not only with manuscript preparation, but also offered professional guidance on secretarial practices.

Ruth Burger was kind enough to permit the use of some interoffice communications of her own, and also lent expert help in the reorganization of the instructional sections.

For permission to use personal material as a basis for model memos, gratitude must be expressed to Jim Lavenson, of the Plaza Hotel; George K. Shumrak, Executive Vice-President of Sweetheart Plastics Inc.; Florence Scharf, Marketing Executive; and to Viking Press for permission to reprint a group of memos, gleaming with the aura of Hollywood stardom, from *Memo From David O. Selznick;* and to *Congressional Quarterly* for Dita Beard's memo.

Many other individuals, both personal friends and professional colleagues, in one way or another offered advice and counsel aimed to increase the effectiveness of this work.

And finally, as every writer knows, somewhere along the road to completion the going gets rocky: fatigue, doubts, and unresolved questions jump out to block progress. In this touch-and-go situation, one's close friends are a major resource, and to these, my gratitude for supplying the emotional reinforcement to persist in and conclude this work.

Auren Uris

Contents

Re: A Memo on Memos

This book is about interoffice memos, the intraorganization messages written by company heads and office boys, by every manager, supervisor, and executive. It's for presidents, vice-presidents, and employees down the line; it's for secretaries, who may want to use this book for themselves or for their boss's sake.

From time to time the vitality of the memo form frees it from its intramural limits. Memos have made front-page news—Dita Beard's message to W. R. Merriam, chief of the International Telephone and Telegraph Company's Washington office, figured in the Watergate investigation. You'll find it on pages 182-183.

A collection of messages by a movie producer appeared in book form—*Memo From David O. Selznick*—and made the best-seller list. The fact that the "employees" talked about are movie stars—Clark Gable, Marlene Dietrich, Vivien Leigh—doesn't detract from our interest. Several of these memos have been included.

Even a recent *New Yorker* cartoon celebrates the form: A cleaning woman in a deserted office is dictating into a tape recorder, "Memo to the Executive Director, Vice-President, Heads of Departments and all members of the staff: 'Wipe your feet.'" Her memo is a model of brevity and directness.

The memo plays a vital function in corporate life. It is this critical role, and its variety of forms as it ebbs and flows through the in- and out-boxes of the land, with which this book is concerned.

Being a flexible communications medium, the memo reflects the complexity of business life—its conflict and harmony, its "businesslikeness," its humanity, and even its politics. In countless interoffice memo files are stored the evidence of the animosities, pains and pleasures, the courage, imagination, creativity, and energy of human beings at work together.

The consequences of the ill-considered or poorly executed memo can show up as dollars lost, time wasted, misunderstandings spawned, and foul-ups caused. There are even legal limitations to memo writing (see the "Dismissal" heading in the sample section, Part II).

The fact is, the ability to write an effective memo is an essential skill. Every manager writes memos. Many write them well, others badly. In between is a large number who falter in grasping the opportunity the form offers to accomplish a range of crucial purposes.

The person who becomes adept at handling the memo not only increases his effectiveness, but also improves his chances for recognition and advancement within his company.

Webster defines the memo as, ". . . a usually brief informal communication typically written for interoffice circulation . . . containing directive, advisory, or informative matter."

This is a serviceable definition and is more or less followed in this work with two modifications:

Although the large majority of memos are brief, recognition is made here of a long version, sometimes referred to as a *report*.

The three types of messages, directive, advisory, and informative, are enlarged to seventy-eight categories, both for comprehensiveness, and for easier finding of specific models.

To the most skilled and sophisticated of managers, writing a memo is not simply a matter of putting words together. The form can be a political device, a weapon no less deadly because the battle is waged on paper (see Politics of the Memo, Section 7). It can be defensive as well as offensive. Jackie Lewis, of *Viva* magazine, was a social psychologist before entering publishing. She was asked if her training was helpful in her work. "Yes," she said, "every day—in replying to interoffice memos."

You don't have to be a social psychologist to handle the memo-writing challenge. The prepared manager can convert situations and problems into opportunities for effectiveness.

This book provides what's needed to improve one's memo-writing skills and is arranged in two sections:

Part I contains a number of chapters designed to help you understand and master the medium.

Part II provides a collection of memo models for almost every occasion and requirement.

The person who masters this medium is vastly strengthened in his quest for status and achievement. This book can go a long way to assist toward those worthy goals.

Signed _Auren Uris_

memos for managers

part i

Section 1

the written word vs. the spoken word

Nobody goes far in the business world today unless he can express himself intelligently on paper. Even in this age of telephones, walkie-talkies, and other oral media, writing remains a major means of communication. There's a good reason. The written word has advantages over the spoken word. Let's examine the most important ones:

Spoken Word

The hearer must get your meaning as you speak.

Once delivered, the message disappears.

You're limited to words and a few simple gestures.

Usually you speak off the cuff.

Written Word

The reader can read and reread until he gets the idea.

What's written can always be kept "for the record."

In addition to words, you can draw diagrams, make charts, add lists, and so on.

You can think through, consider, and reconsider your message.

This is not to say that the spoken word never has advantages. There are occasions when it's useful to be able to see the hearer's reactions, elaborate a point that seems to puzzle him, answer his questions. Nevertheless, under the pressures of business today, every executive must learn to communicate by means of the written word, to ask questions, answer them, make statements, describe plans, and so on.

Especially to be avoided is the sudden substitution of memos for oral exchanges. For example: Executive Peter Miller comes in one morning and finds his in-box loaded with memos from his boss, some on subjects usually dealt with during informal meetings. "Good lord!" says Peter. "The boss is mad at me!" Eventually Pete's superior explains that he just wanted "to get his thinking down on paper while it was fresh," and Pete feels better about the whole thing.

But let's not mince words. Most of us find it a lot easier to talk than to write. One executive confesses, "I can give an oral report to my boss without the slightest problem. But when he tells me, 'Put it in writing,' I sweat bullets with every page."

For many people, writing is an awkward medium. Yet, by mastering a few simple points, even a self-conscious writer can develop the confidence to do himself justice on paper.

It can be helpful to stand back and view yourself in terms of the broader perspective of your role in the company for which you work. Every executive, no matter what his title, has a personal communications network that functions within the company system. This network can be presented by a diagram:

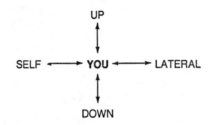

PERSONAL COMMUNICATIONS NETWORK

An executive may communicate heavily in some directions, sparsely in others. For example, a sales manager may find that 90 percent of his outgoing correspondence is addressed to his salesmen, the remaining 10 percent in other organizational directions. On the other hand, a company treasurer may find that most of his communication involves up-the-line correspondence with relatively few contacts down the line.

Just a brief word about the situation suggested by the left-hand element in the diagram. In addition to communication in the three directions shown, we may send messages to ourselves, usually as reminders: "Contact JC Monday morning about the Jones matter" reads a note on an executive's own desk pad. It can be an important part of one's memo-writing network, and some samples of the category will be found under the "Reminders to Oneself" heading, Part II.

MEMOS AMONG THE MEDIA

There are three ways of communicating:
- Face-to-face contact, either one-to-one or as in conferences and meetings.
- The written word—memos, lengthy reports, and so on.
- Telephone and other electrical devices; recorders, radio, TV.

In practice, each of the basic media has advantages and disadvantages. The chart below helps clarify the pros and cons of each form. The formal report has been given separate consideration here because its length and scope set it somewhat apart from the memo, which tends to be briefer and plays a somewhat different role in the media scheme of things.

Method	Advantages	Disadvantages
Phone	Speed. Permits give and take of questions.	Words and figures might be misunderstood or garbled. Usually no record of conversation. May be an interruption of ongoing work.
In Person	Visual. You can "show" and "explain." In many cases permits better meeting of the minds.	You may have to leave your work area, lose "travel time." The time may be inconvenient to you *or* the other person.
Informal Note or Memo	Brief. It and copies can be filed "for the record." Permits considered statement. Greater impact than spoken word.	You don't get an immediate reply. Your memo is at the mercy of a routine delivery and the bulk of the receiver's mail, or his disinclination to tap his in-box.
Formal Report	Complete. Permits time for organization of material. Can be reported to others. Authoritative.	Sometimes requires considerable time. May make for slow reading at receiver's end. Particularly susceptible to problems of organization and presentation.

IMPORTANCE OF THE MEMO

There are certain situations in which any one of the three basic communications media might do the job. For example, one may make an announcement or ask a question by phone, face-to-face, or by memo. The choice may be a matter of personal preference or convenience. But there are types of message and usage for which the memo is unsurpassed.

As the previous chart suggests, the memo has unique advantages when the objective is: record-keeping, permanence, the special impact of "getting it in writing."

The written message has these additional virtues:

• A secretary who types her boss's memos is kept up-to-date on his activities—which wouldn't be the case with face-to-face or phone transactions.

• By copying-in others, you can inform an entire group of a particular matter—unlike a phone call, and unlike a meeting, which might yield no record.

• A copy of a memo in a follow-up file can assure a check to see what's been done on a particular matter.

• In long-distance communication, as between two far-removed branches of a company, a written message isn't subject to mail delay, but can be transmitted by facsimile—a message of four lines can be transmitted in one minute by a telecopier.

In addition, there are a host of nuance effects of the memo that are less obvious, but can be crucial: the "political" aspects of memo writing, for example (see Section 7).

Here are some typical situations in which a memo probably deserves to be the medium of choice:

To	Subject	Purpose
General foreman	Overages	To call attention to an undesirable practice
All divisional foremen	Report of Service Dept.	To tell production people how they're doing
Head of R&D	Description of a product need	To start thinking about a new and salable product
All divisional employees	Quarterly production report	To inform employees, build "team" sense
Company president	Company house organ	To comment favorably on company communication
Head of Quality Control	Reject percentages	To ask for a meeting
Sales manager	Visit of a prospective customer to plant	To inform sales head
Cashier's office	Travel expenses	To complete an internal financial transaction
Any employee	Personal messages	Congratulations, praise, condolences, good wishes, encouragement, etc.

MASTERING THE SKILL

The memo is both *actually* simple and *deceptively* simple. Writing a memo is a little like skiing: Anyone can strap himself onto a pair of skis. But there is considerable difference in the man who just stands there and the skier who zips down the steep slopes with speed, verve, and pleasure.

The manager who is familiar with the world of the memo in all its variety is in a much stronger position to make his mark than the one for whom the writing of a memo is a mystery and the writing of a good memo a minor miracle.

For some people in business, Section 9, "Writing the Long Report," will be of particular value in improving overall writing skills. The next section zeroes in on the special qualities of the memo and further explains its vitality and impact.

Section 2

the memo as tool and trumpet

Writing is a highly personal matter. The memo that goes out over your name is as revealing as the clothes you wear or the quality of your handwriting. Every time you send out a memo to your boss, a colleague, or your subordinates, you demonstrate the way you think, your vocabulary, the way you organize your ideas. If you're writing to strangers, your memos, for better or worse, are your introduction.

A memo may suggest that a person is clever, knows what he's talking about, has a good sense of humor, thinks clearly; or, that he is dull, stuffy, and doesn't know much.

Being personal, the memo can be profound or superficial, moving or insensitive, pompous or portentous, silly or wise. That may be more revealing than most people want to be.

One executive says, "If you want to know the kind of manager a man is, go through the file of memos he's written."

WHY A MEMO IS MORE THAN "JUST A TOOL"

In rounding up the sample memos reproduced in Part II, we discovered that many managers were reluctant to open up their files. "My memos show me with my shirttails out" is the way one manager put it as he apologized for turning down our request. Fortunately, many granted permission and simply asked for anonymity.

However, the experience did highlight one important fact. These executives were confirming the fact that when you write a memo to someone in your company, you're doing at least three things:

• You're moving ahead on the subject of the communication itself.

• You're showing your degree of mastery of one of the most important management skills—the ability to put thoughts in writing.

• You're exposing your personality—the kind of person you are.

To put it another way, you're using an everyday business tool and—for better or for worse—trumpeting your skill before your associates. No wonder so many managers get stagefright!

THE MEMO AS PERSONAL SHOWCASE

Above and beyond its purely business function, the memo is, of course, also a literary form. It has its techniques, its aesthetic and emotional impacts. While the memo lacks the sweep of the novel and the delicate imagery of poetry, it does have the power to inspire, enlighten, inform, excite, and encourage.

The memo is a natural executive métier. The manager who is an *auteur manqué* finds in the memo a great opportunity to address an audience. All his literary creativity can find an outlet here—his pet words and phrases, his wit and humor, his need to express his feelings. Occasionally memos are of such cogency that they are copied and circulated like a benign version of the secret Russian underground press.

Like a true art form, the memo has range and flexibility. It can be as simple as a one-word answer, assume architectural grandeur in the form of a multi-page report.

It can be as public as a message addressed "To All Employees," as private as a highly personal and confidential note to a colleague.

It may be as innocuous as a statement that, "Starting Monday, the company library will be open for use at 9 A.M.," or as supercharged as a description of a new product that would be worth millions to a competitor.

DEVELOPING YOUR REPUTATION

Since the memo can be highly personal, your own output is always adding to your personal portrait. Reputations are not made—or lost—on the basis of a single communication, as a rule. But, over a period of time, a pattern is bound to emerge.

If you doubt that fact, just examine a six-month accumulation of carbons, either your own or someone else's. You will be amazed to see the repetition of words and phrases, the similarity of tone and/or style.

Obviously, the difference in subject matter of the memos will dictate some differences. But, on the other hand, you may notice that since your communications with certain people tend to be on the same type of subject, your memos to any one individual also have a tendency to have similar qualities. This is not *necessarily* bad, but it *can be*.

For example, it doesn't matter much if your announcements of meetings or brief routine notes are short, dry, and to the point. However, you would probably not want all your important up-the-line communications to reflect a Johnny-one-note tone. If you recognize that your memos may be perceived as personal "sales presentations," you will see the value of shaping them to do your credit. It may take a little more time—and just a little more thought—but it's your own career that you're investing in.

FINDING THE TIME TO DO IT RIGHT

Memo writing is, after all, only one part of the executive workload. The percentage of time it requires can vary considerably. Some executives get by with one or two memos a week; others turn out dozens a day.

Just like any other part of the executive schedule, memo writing must be fitted in to a suitable part of the overall work pattern. Some common practices:

Morning start

Some managers begin the day by taking care of their paper work. This may include not only intraorganizational messages but also outside letters. There are usually two justifications for this timing. One is that it's often a low-pressure period in an executive's schedule. Another factor: morning delivery of the mail is a natural starter, since the influx must be screened to take care of high-priority material.

Workday's end

Some memo writers find that their work schedule eases toward the end of the day. (This is not to suggest that memo writing is a low-priority item to be fitted in when convenient, but that other "do" items may involve one's boss or subordinates, who depend on immediate response to their needs.)

Another point favoring end-of-day memo writing: the affairs of the day may themselves require covering, one way or another, by memo.

For people who use this timing and have a secretary, one caution: avoid end-of-day dictation that will require working overtime. An emergency may justify this practice occasionally, but otherwise it's likely to be seen as an imposition—and resented.

It's usually more efficient for like activities to be bunched. Communications, both incoming and outgoing, taken care of, can clear the decks for other things. Bunching also nullifies the need for starts and stops that are themselves time-consuming.

Of course, there are no absolute rules here and situations can alter practices. Some executives may find it better to fit in their memo writing between other activities.

Another element of timing is not necessarily within the control of the executive. It depends on the pickup and delivery schedules set by the mailroom. When a memo message is of urgent nature, the executive may want to arrange for memo delivery independent of regular mail routines.

Section 3

practices that make perfect

Many forms and conventions have been developed that aim for convenience, quick comprehension, and fewer errors. Case in point: the physical form of the memo, of which there are many versions. Basically, however, there are two. One is the company's own interoffice form. Here's a sample:

EFG Company

INTEROFFICE MEMO

To_____

From_____

Date_____

Subject_____

The other form is an individual one, which some companies provide, or which the manager gets for himself from a local printer. This form tends to be quite simple and may bear some printed legend, such as "From the Desk of . . ." and the name of the manager, or simply the word "Memo." This is an area where some managers give their imaginations free rein. Accordingly, you sometimes see memo forms with busy little figures rushing around smoking at the heels, flying Mercurys, sheets of paper being propelled by beating wings, and so on. Each to his own taste. Another variation is the company name with the suffix *-gram* added; for example, the Ray-o-gram (for the Ray Company).

The company's interoffice memo is usually typed by a secretary or typist, whereas the personal memo (From the Desk of . . .) is more often handwritten by the manager or executive. In some organizations, memos are given distinction by a color code; for example, the weekly communication in which a sales manager gives sales figures to his men in the field is printed on green, expense forms are yellow, and so on. This can help easier identification at both sending and receiving ends. For repetitive messages of some importance, it may be helpful to use color coding to make it easy for the recipient to pick the message out of a pile of other correspondence.

13

Other needs, other forms. The great flexibility of the memo shows itself by numerous variations. In some cases the efficiency of the memo exchange is helped by write-in answers tailored into the original form. Note this executive's memo to his staff:

Frank Amster, vice-president of Kayline Products, will be paying us a visit on Friday, January 21. He would like to meet key people in engineering and production. Please indicate below what time period would suit your schedule best:

☐ between 11 A.M. and 12 noon
☐ lunch
☐ between 1:30 and 2:30 P.M.
☐ between 2:30 and 3:30 P.M.
Other?_____

Soon as possible, please.

Pat Masters

This "self-mailer" technique is particularly useful when:
• You want to obtain fast replies from others within the department or within the company.
• You need 100 percent response. Most people tend to complete a fast check-off form more easily than one that involves the time and thought that goes into an open-ended reply.
• You are asking a number of people the same question. It then becomes easier to tabulate the responses, or plan a schedule, as shown in the example above.
• The answers you're looking for can be *categorized* ("Yes," "No," for example) or put in *numerical form* (0–25, 26–50, 51–75, and so on).

Another form that tends to increase the likelihood and speed of a reply is one that can be purchased from almost any stationery store. This typically consists of a two-part form with carbons. The sender fills out the top part of the form, then tears out a carbon for his record. The recipient gets the original message and a tear-off portion of the sheet on which he can send his answer. An additional carbon records his comment so that he is now left with the original memo and a carbon of his reply as a record.

In addition to forms, there are practices which add still further to the memo's flexibility. A perfectly complete and acceptable message may be a single word scrawled over someone's query and returned to the sender. At the other end of the scale is the formal memo, with such notations as AU:WM.

The first letters are the initials of the sender of the memo, the second pair, of the person who has prepared and typed the message.

cc:John Doe
Jane Doe
etc.

This notes the people other than the direct recipient who have received carbon copies of the message. In these days of copying machines, this indication may be *xc,* x for Xerox, or other letter indicating the nature of the copier.

The indication *bcc:* goes only on the file copy of the memo and notes the fact that "blind" copies have been sent to John Roe, Mary Roe, etc., but this fact is not noted for the recipient.

The whole matter of who gets copies of memos is treated in detail in Section 6, Copies to . . . or, Who Gets the Copies?

MEMO TO A GROUP

When there is to be a meeting, the sender of the memo may want to make assignments to a number of individual participants. These notes may be handwritten or typed on the copy going to that particular individual and need not appear on those of the other memo recipients. Be sure that your file copy indicates the additional notes—handwritten or typed—and the names of each of the recipients alongside the special assignment. You can use your file copy to check the assignments after they have been fulfilled, and for further follow-up when necessary.

In cases where a memo is to be sent to a group of people, a matter of protocol arises: In what sequence should the names of the recipients be arranged? This may seem like a minor matter but it seldom is where personal status is involved. The most generally accepted way of handling this matter is to list names alphabetically. However, when among the recipients there is a person of notably higher status—for example, as there would be in a board of directors—this person should head the list and the other names be arranged in alphabetical order.

FILING YOUR MEMOS

A broad range of methods for filing memos was revealed in checking with a number of executive secretaries. Generally, the system used—in most cases designed and maintained by the secretary—depends on the needs of the individual executive.

In individual cases the best filing approach depends on specific factors. Since there may be a difference in filing requirements for incoming and outgoing messages, they deserve separate consideration.

Incoming

Here are the factors which influence the method to be used:

QUANTITY?   The question of the number of memos you receive breaks down into two aspects. The first, the total number of memos you receive in an average day or week, is less important than the second, the number that *deserve to be kept.* It's wise to discard as much of the incoming flow as possible.

The percentage of "keepables" may range from none to 100 percent. To decide which memos to keep and which to discard, it helps to remind yourself as to why memos deserve to be retained. Here are three good reasons:

For the record.   Your boss sends you a memo telling you that he's putting you in charge of hand-tool requisitions. Any supervisor who wants to purchase hand tools must clear it with you. You hold on to this statement in case a question arises as to your authority in this matter.

Also "For the record" are those memos which may have political implications. For example, an executive gets a memo from a colleague voicing his strong disagreement with a company policy. This can be a source of trouble, especially if it falls into the wrong hands. For political reasons it may be helpful to the recipient to be able to produce that memo as a clincher in an argument or as a bit of pertinent history. Such memos naturally belong in the keepable category, simply for protective purposes.

Information source.   The engineering department sends you a report telling you the dates on which a serviceman from an equipment supplier will be available. You keep this type of message for ready referral to the facts it contains.

Matters of sentiment.   The president of the company sends you a personal message of congratulations for bringing a tough project to a successful conclusion. You want to hold on to that as a symbol and reminder of victory.

If none of these reasons pertain, it's likely that the memo can be read, acted on, and discarded, which slims down the record-keeping chore.

Outgoing

The factors that determine which of your outgoing memos you keep copies of are similar to the reasons for holding on to incoming correspondence. For example, you'll keep a copy of a memo you've written as a record of a statement, an agreement, or the specific wording of a directive you have issued.

And, of course, your own memos carry information to which you yourself may want to refer. If you have submitted a report to your boss on the output of your department for the past quarter, it's not unlikely that you yourself may want to check back on these figures and attendant facts in the future.

And even your sentimental messages or those having some special personal quality may deserve to be saved in duplicate in your files. Sometimes an executive saves his memos of congratulations, praise, and so on, so that he'll be sure to vary the wording on a subsequent occasion.

Once the executive has worked out the pattern of his memo-saving he has an idea of the extensiveness of the files he'll need. For the most part there's a tendency to segregate interoffice material from outside correspondence—usually by the simple expedient of having a separate drawer or perhaps an entire separate standing file for this purpose.

Here are some of the possibilities:

• **THE SINGLE FILE.**   One executive whose memo-load is rather slim and whose matter-of-factness about messages makes it possible for him to cut down drastically on the number of those retained uses just a single file folder marked "Interoffice." As his secretary files the memos she simply puts them in chronological order, the newest toward the front of the file. With one file folder for incoming and the other for outgoing memos, this executive's filing system is perfectly satisfactory.

• **SUBJECT FILE.** An engineering executive who has voluminous internal correspondence on a number of different projects feels his records must be complete, and so he discards nothing. In order to accommodate the volume of memos and to make the material available as needed he organizes his file folders according to subject: "Acme Project," "Atlanta Project," "New Wing," etc.

• **ALPHABETICAL FILE.** For managers with heavy patterns of interoffice correspondence, filing by name of the memo-sender or recipient is appropriate. For example, a purchasing agent who has correspondence with a number of top- and middle-management executives keeps his memos alphabetized under the names of individual executives.

In some situations executives—or their secretaries—use a combination of the three methods described above. That is, they may have a chronological file and, for memos that relate to a special major subject, a subject file. Unfortunately the systems used to file intraorganizational communications tend to be more haphazard than those used for regular correspondence. In part this is because there is less ambiguity about the reasons for retaining outside correspondence. Letters from customers, suppliers, and so on, often must be kept for the record and for legal, contractual, and related purposes. The informality of much memo correspondence makes saving it more questionable, and therefore the filing system tends to be more flexible, to put it euphemistically. The comparison shows up in the remarks of one secretary, who said, "My outside correspondence is filed very neatly and efficiently. The interoffice files are a mess."

Of course, the purpose of filing is not for filing's sake but for retrieval. As long as it's desirable to hold on to memos and to make it relatively simple to retrieve specific ones, it's worth systematizing your memo-keeping practices.

Tickler File

Memos have the same "tickling" requirements that outside correspondence does. If your boss sends you a memo telling you that he's set up a meeting for you with another executive, you want a reminder of this future event, and the memo is "tickled"—that is, so handled that it will come to your attention in time to remind you of the meeting.

Generally, a tickler file is kept separately as a source of follow-up, day by day. Each folder should be headed by the name of the month, and the correspondence, with target dates indicated on each memo, placed in the folder according to priorities for that particular month. Such a system is vitally important to managers and executives, and merely noting such a follow-up on a desk calendar or worksheet does not promote efficiency in finding, for example, a memo written on June 1 with a follow-up noted on top for say, July 1. If the memo is kept in an ordinary file, and correspondence is heavy, a lot of time could be wasted wading through the file to find that particular memo, especially if time is of the essence. Retaining such a memo in the monthly tickler file makes it more readily available.

In some cases, a date for future action noted in a memo is "tickled" by being put on a desk calendar or worksheet. If the original memo may be needed, its location should likewise be noted so that it can be retrieved from the files.

When a memo in the tickler file has been acted upon and requires future referral or revisions, it should be retained in a file folder in the appropriate filing cabinet. In some cases, of course, when no further action or referral will be necessary, the correspondence may be discarded.

Section 4 how to dictate

Executives save precious hours and a great deal of inconvenience by dictating their memos. With the aid of a stenographer or dictating machine, they zip through outgoing correspondence that might otherwise take two or three times as long.

But some executives do not dictate either because they have tried and failed or have never tried. In some cases the deterrent is a form of mike fright. Confronted by the *need* to speak, even a fluent speaker may freeze. Whatever the problem, the final feeling is that dictation is not for them. Thus they scribble longhand notes to be handed over to a secretary, or write out their correspondence in full and then have a typist transcribe it, or they peck their way through correspondence by doing their own typing.

Dictation, however, is by far the most efficient method for handling outgoing correspondence. There's no doubt that the executive who can dictate—not only letters, but *anything* that is to appear in writing—can save himself hours of toil. And for anyone who wants to make it in print, learning to dictate can be a major step forward. Those who dictate well can tell you that timesaving isn't the only benefit. In the words of one executive: "I can think more clearly as well as express myself more efficiently when I dictate than when I write."

Writers love to tell the story of one of the most popular authors of the 1930s. He was the envy of the profession. Love stories, detective stories, adventure stories, Westerns—they flowed from his brain into the magazine market in a never-ending stream. As a result of this fertility, he amassed a tidy fortune.

The secret of his ability to turn out short stories like sausages lay largely in one fact: he dictated his copy. Legend has it that he spent his time cruising off the Florida coast in a yacht stocked with food, drink, and a half dozen stenographers to whom he would dictate in turn.

BECOMING A GREAT DICTATOR

Anyone who can speak can dictate. Ironically, many managers who don't consider themselves "dictators" nevertheless are. For example: Manager Pete Bramble, holding a query he has just received from the Front Office, gets his boss's secretary to take a letter. He says, "All right, Gladys, here it is: To Mr. C. R. Castor. Dear Mr. Castor, colon. In reply to your question about the drums piled up in the hallway of Building B, comma, I'm happy to report that they've just been removed, period. Signed, Pete Bramble." He doesn't have to bother adding the date or address. Gladys will take care of that.

But suggest to Pete Bramble that he dictate a five-page report and he'll say, "Can't do it," believing the statement to be self-explanatory. Everybody knows *lengthy* communications of any substance must be drafted in longhand, or pecked out on a type-writer. But, in this case, what "everybody knows" is false. Practically any executive can become reasonably good at dictating, good enough to cut his writing time by 50 percent, or even more.

Consider Pete Bramble's case, and that of anyone else who's dictation-shy. The secret of a breakthrough lies in *gradualism.*

Pete had no trouble with *short* memos. OK, so the thing to do is start with the brief messages that consist of one or two sentences, a paragraph or two. (Do the longer ones the way they've always been done—whichever way it is.)

Stick to these simple memos, dictating away until your confidence has begun to firm up. Then, gradually, dictate longer ones, three or four paragraphs. The fact will soon emerge that in longer ones it's difficult to sustain the thought. But this problem can be overcome by jotting down your ideas in advance, using key words and phrases. Armed with this outline, the dictation will proceed smoothly.

As one builds confidence and strengthens his technique, accomplishment grows —and one's status as a dictator is established.

The benefits potential of dictation is demonstrated by these figures: the executive who writes a 600-word report in longhand can produce the finished product in about one hour. If he dictates to a capable stenographer he probably can cut the time to a third, or twenty minutes. If he uses a dictating machine, he can get his thoughts down almost as quickly as he can find the words for them.

The advantages of being able to dictate are so enormous that every executive owes it to himself to at least give the technique a try. Obviously some people will be more successful than others.

Interestingly, it isn't always the fluent speaker who makes the best dictator. The person who is less fluent and even stumbles over words may actually dictate "harder" (as opposed to rambling) copy. If one's thinking is orderly, dictation may be more concise than that of a person who speaks easily but whose thoughts meander.

SEVEN STEPS TO VICTORY

To help improve your dictating skill, study these seven points:

1. What to dictate

While almost anything *can* be dictated, it doesn't follow that you'll want to dictate all communications. For example, dictation won't save any time on short lists of words or phrases. The longer the writing job, the greater the potential saving.

Memos are prime candidates for dictation. A trained secretary can often compose an entire message when the boss dictates one or two key sentences, leaving the formalities of address, salutation, and closing to be filled in.

2. Stenographer or machine

You may have a choice between using a stenographer or a dictating machine. In recent years, dictating equipment has been greatly improved and refined. Machines are lighter, easier to operate. Some companies have centralized dictation systems, so that an executive simply picks up the telephone when he wants to dictate, dials a special number, and talks. The receiving device, at a remote centralized location, records the dictation. The tape is later transcribed by someone in a typing pool.

The approach just described has come to be known as Word Processing. A likely consequence of Word Processing is the elimination of the stenographer and secretary. At present, however, it's pretty much a large-company concept. And even though the ranks of the secretary may thin out for technological reasons, chances are it's an employee category that will persist—along with that of the executive.

At any rate, the contemporary manager may have the choice between a dictating machine and a stenographer. Each has advantages and disadvantages which should be considered in selecting the most suitable method. The following chart compares the two:

	Advantages	**Disadvantages**
Dictating Machine	Doesn't complain; has no personal habits or traits to disturb you (although it *can* get out of order).	Can lend itself to corrections, but some managers find a machine more difficult in this aspect.
	Available anytime during the day, 24 hours a day.	If transcriber has difficulty discerning words or phrases dictated, the dictator may not always be available to be asked. He may also forget what he said.
	Is tireless.	
	Some people are less self-conscious when they dictate to a machine.	Transcriber might feel it's a waste of time to listen first to the entire recording before typing. It may seem more advantageous to take it down in shorthand to facilitate transcription. (This would apply to corrections, changes, determining punctuation, and would add to transcription time.)
	Can be taken home for the weekend —without complications.	
Stenographer	Good rapport between stenographer and dictator aids dictation.	Usually works eight-hour day, may resist overtime.
	Corrections, insertions, changes can be made on the spot; readbacks are helpful in organizing thoughts.	May tire after an hour or so.
		If steno is absent from work and has not completed transcription of her

	Advantages	**Disadvantages**
Stenographer	Can help by giving instant feedback in terms of reaction to pace of work, ideas, etc.	notes, chances are no substitute can read her shorthand. This means a delay until steno returns to work.
		Requires care, regular feeding, consideration as a non-robot. (This may also be an advantage.)

3. Organize your ideas

The single most important step in learning to dictate has nothing to do with dictation. Many executives conclude they are poor dictators because they attempt the near-impossible—organizing their material while speaking. Obviously, short letters and memos can often be dictated off the top of the head. But this isn't true for long reports, complicated material, or a presentation that requires a logical structure and specific details.

Many people cling to longhand because they can stop, think, and organize as they write. Dictation by no means short-cuts preparation of the material, and it may require even more careful planning. But the end result is often better than writing if you follow these two steps in getting ready:

• **COLLECT ALL INFORMATION,** reference material, exhibits, and so on. Also, arrange background material in the order in which it is to be used. Once dictating starts, you shouldn't have to interrupt yourself to search for a missing piece of information.

• **MAKE A ROUGH OUTLINE.** An outline provides a track to run on, a framework to build the final product. It needn't be elaborate. A few words or phrases to give a logical sequence of ideas will do the trick. For example, this section was dictated on the basis of the following notes:

> Introduction: dictation as a timesaver
> Other benefits and problems
> Everyone can do it to some degree
> Practice helps
> 1. What to dictate
> 2. Stenographer or machine
> 3. Organize your ideas
> 4. Getting started
> 5. Sustaining the effort
> 6. Improving your copy
> 7. Improving your technique
> Conclusion

Other preparations such as physical arrangements for convenient working—a comfortable chair, a table or desk for notes and background materials, a comfortable location for your stenographer, if you are using one, or a good spot for your dictating apparatus—round out the preparatory steps.

4. Getting started

"I just can't get off the ground," confesses one executive in explaining why he doesn't like to dictate.

It's a common problem. Many people, including experienced professional writers, often develop the jitters at the starting gate. However, there are several tricks that can help beat "writer's block:"

a. Check back and make sure all preparations have been made. In some cases, the feelings of not being ready to dictate may be the obstacle.

b. *Start!* Throw caution and hesitation to the winds. Don't worry about finding the "right" word, phrase, or sentence. Plunge in! In other words, an effective way to end a "starting" problem is simply to *begin.* And begin with a brief or "easy" piece of dictation. This is a trick often used by experienced dictators who have starting trouble.

5. Sustaining the effort

You've been dictating for five or ten minutes. Then you stop and you can't seem to pick up the thread. How do you keep going? Discussions with executives reveal several common *hangups:*

• "I can't get down to fundamentals, I ramble and digress." The answer here lies both in having and *following* an outline. If you find you're straying from it, go over it to make sure it covers your subject adequately. Then, stick to it, *forcing* yourself to veer away from any digression.

• "It makes me nervous to have a stenographer waiting for me to finish a sentence." Nothing is more disconcerting than an impatient stenographer. If you aren't blessed with one that has a placid, understanding nature, try using a dictating machine —or change stenographers. Or tell your stenographer at the outset that you don't expect to talk smoothly and incessantly and that she must expect to wait for you to gather your thoughts or seek the word or phrase you want. Make it clear that interruptions are a standard part of the procedure—at least, your procedure.

• "I don't like gadgets, and talking to a lifeless machine is disquieting." (Some executives have the opposite hangup.) The obvious step—try a stenographer. Also, investigate a different machine. The one being used may be a poor choice for you. In today's market, there's a wide variety of equipment. If you are having trouble, a trip to an office supply company will make it possible to test out a variety of machines. You should be able to come up with one that suits you better.

• "I lose too much time searching for a word or phrase or even an idea." This is a common and major hangup for many people. The answer is simple—put down any word or phrase that will get you over the hurdle, remembering that it's easy enough to make changes on the typed copy later.

The important thing is to work for a rough draft. Once you get your thoughts down in black and white, you have something to work with. The professional writer will push on to complete his draft regardless of how many word gaps or idea gaps there may be in his copy. He knows that the weaknesses can be rectified in a second pass.

• "I find it impossible to sustain effort on a long draft." If you are working on a difficult report, don't try to complete the draft in one sitting. Break the outline down into pieces and regard each part as a report in itself. Dictation requires concentration and each person must determine how long he can work without undue physical or mental fatigue. Don't go beyond the point where you feel you're pushing a rock up a mountain.

6. Improving your copy

The greatest misconception about dictation is that once it's transcribed that finishes the job. Seldom is dictated or written copy "right" the first time. Every professional writer will tell you that it's the *rewriting* that makes the copy "sing."

So consider the typed pages you get back from the typist as merely a draft, a preliminary version. Then sit down with your pencil and give your copy shape. If you succeed in turning your first rewrite into what professional writers call "final copy," excellent. But don't get discouraged if it takes two or even three rewrites before you're pleased with the final product.

In the editing or rewriting, you can eliminate objectionable mannerisms. For example, watch for repetition of such phrases as "in fact" or "to be sure," which go unnoticed in verbal communication but which become objectionable in writing. Count on your editing to eliminate and tighten up. Below are "before" and "after" paragraphs indicating how this is done.

There's no doubt that the man—manager, technician, executive—anyone who can dictate not only letters but almost anything that is to appear in black and white—can save himself hours of toil often required by business writing. This article tells you how to develop the ability to dictate anything. For anyone who wants to make it in print, learning to dictate can be a major step forward in a timesaving "writing" skill.

The manager, technician, executive, who can dictate can save considerable time. This article tells you how to develop the ability to dictate anything. For those who want to make it in print, learning to dictate can be a major step forward.

7. Improving your technique

After you have tried dictating once or twice, review your experience. Where did you get hung up? Where does your technique need improvement? Here are some suggestions that may help you:

PRACTICE. This is crucial. There is no known case record of an executive, even one experienced in dictating, undertaking long pieces without some preliminary difficulties. While practice may not always make perfect, it does make for improvement.

SPOT YOUR WEAK POINTS. There are undoubtedly some aspects of dictation you do well, others less so. For example, one executive found that he could talk smoothly and continuously. However, when his dictation had been transcribed, he discovered that he had wandered from his subject. This meant that a considerable amount of copy had to be cut. Accordingly, in his later dictation he made a special effort to write out and adhere to his outline.

A second executive had the opposite problem. He stuck closer to his outline but found that his words came slowly and hesitantly. His solution: more time spent thinking about the subject and elaborating the outline—the sub-points and sub-sub-points, as well as major elements.

If first attempts are discouraging, try again, using material of which you have a good grasp. Don't give up too quickly, because the rewards of success can be substantial. And repeated attempts are sure to help score a breakthrough.

Although timesaving is the most obvious benefit, some dictators claim that the *quality* of their writing improves when they dictate: "I find that I can express myself more naturally when I talk than when I type or write out my ideas in longhand," says one manager. "The final result is less stilted, even more imaginative."

You may be the greatest dictator of all times, but you won't know unless you polish your skill to its full potential.

Section 5

hazards
and pitfalls

The memo is susceptible to abuse and misuse. And since it exists in the real world, real damage may result when there is a misfire. For example, enmity between colleagues may grow out of a "that-isn't-what-I-meant" memo. Serious demoralization may strike an entire organization because of a poorly worded message from the top. Here are the kinds of problems that can have undesirable consequences:

Garbled, or misleading facts

One manager writes to another that "there have been countless instances where people from your department have interfered with the work in my area, sometimes leading to serious disruptions." The kindest thing that could be said of this statement is that it's not a lie but an exaggeration. There have, in fact, been just one or two minor difficulties. Unless a memo writer is looking for trouble, efforts must be made to keep statements of fact clear, constructive, and cogent.

Unclear writing

A company president sends a message to all employees announcing a plan to "rehabilitate" one of the buildings in the plant. Because some people do not understand the meaning of the word *rehabilitate,* and the memo does nothing to contradict rumors that are rife on the grapevine, employees are led to believe that the building will be shut down permanently. Near panic ensues.

Especially in a message "To All Employees," absolute simplicity and clarity are essential because of the broad range of intelligence and education represented, and the likelihood of confusion caused by static from other sources. But, of course, clarity is advisable no matter who's at the receiving end. The reader has only your words on paper to convey the message. If the words aren't right, the message cannot be properly understood.

Unfortunately, fuzzy writing is fairly common on the business scene. Much of it can be avoided if the writer makes a point of using the simplest words and phrases rather than the vague high-flown and unnecessarily inflated ones. The samples below make the point:

Fuzzy	Preferred
"At the present time"	"At present" or "Now"
"one and the same"	"the same"
"It's inconceivable"	"Perhaps" or "Maybe"
"had intended to"	"meant"
"If and when"	"If"
"I deem it advisable"	"It's advisable"
"It is with regret that"	"I regret"
"an insufficiency of"	"not enough"
"It is with considerable pleasure that"	"I'm happy to"
"As I sat down at my desk today, I thought to myself"	Skip it and get down to business

Jargon

In some cases an "in" word unfamiliar to the recipient, or a word or phrase not generally understood, will bewilder rather than inform. Here, for example, is a message sent out by a personnel department to employees:

> The 1974 WDW cards have arrived. You may now proceed with the request forms. Thank you.

Of the twenty people receiving this message, six had to contact the personnel department to ask, "What's a WDW card?"

Some managers cope with the problem of intelligibility by asking secretaries or other people to read a draft. Where the message is particularly important this is a wise precaution; the reader will ask about unclear words or passages.

Misreading

The state of mind or the reading habits of the recipient may lead to his missing the point, or a point, of a message: "How come my department wasn't included in the list of those making its quota?" demands a supervisor. "It was," replies his boss, "right on the second page," which the supervisor neglected to read.

Individuals whose comprehension quotient from reading material is low may require personal follow-ups. But in most cases, good use of emphasis devices—separate paragraphs for each item, numbering, underlining—minimizes most of the hazard. Some managers personalize a message by underlining a key word or phrase, and writing a comment on the memo—"This is your assignment, Bill," or, "Note changed time."

Unwise delegation

Some managers with good language ability and at ease with the written word, risk losing out on the opportunities that good memo writing offers by permitting either their secretary or subordinate to take over their memo duties. In many cases this is perfectly acceptable: No reason why your secretary, for example, shouldn't send out a memo over your signature that says, "The new product task force will meet in the conference room next Monday at 10 o'clock."

If that's all there is to the memo, it would be unwise for the executive not to have his secretary put out this brief item for him. But there are two pitfalls: Both parties may be embarrassed if the item needs redoing. And if the executive lets the unsatisfactory memo go "as is," it is his reputation that's on the line.

Remember, a memo is personal—the quality of one's thinking, language, etc., shows. It is unwise to delegate this activity unless long experience suggests that there will be no regrets.

Sending off a memo unread

Even if you dictate all memos yourself, each memo deserves a final review because there are a number of mistakes that may crop up, any of which can make trouble:

It may go to the wrong person.

A memo sent to a group of people may omit an intended recipient who might very well be upset by the apparent slight.

A fact or a figure may not be accurately stated.

It's up to the sender to check to prevent errors which may be extremely serious. At least, key tables, lists, and so on should be reviewed.

Errors, typographical or otherwise, may fog the message.

And, reading the message may suggest an addition, or a worthwhile afterthought.

However, for ordinary messages, an exception may be made by using a traditional practice. In this case, an executive in haste may ask his secretary to send a message adding the note, "Dictated but not read." Not flattering to the recipient, perhaps, but it does suggest that the writer has made the choice between delay and rapid delivery. This procedure is recommended for uncrucial matters only.

Bureaucratese

It's typical of large organizations—the government is a prime example—that information memos must be sent out notifying somebody of something. Here's the kind of memo that can cause strong men to weep (with laughter) because of its seeming inanity; this one was sent out by a department of a state government:

> On January 18, 1973 I issued a memorandum concerning reimbursement for round trips of less than 35 miles. In the memorandum, I indicated that we would allow reimbursement for round trips of 35 miles or less at the rate of $ .08294 with no additional reimbursement for tolls or parking. It was our understanding that the $ .08294 rate was established and required by the Department of Audit and Control.
>
> Thanks to the persistence of one of our Bureau Chiefs, we have found that the Department of Audit and Control officially does not require the rate to be carried to the 5th decimal place. They have indicated that we may use $ .083 instead. Therefore, in the future please use the $ .083 rate.

Unfortunately, there is not too much that can be done to stop the flow of such information memos. They are characteristic of organization needs, rather than a flaw in the memo medium.

Sometimes the problem can be ameliorated by massing detailed information. Instead of a succession of memos about minutiae, put them all in a single message, or a manual.

And perhaps a modicum of humor can brighten the message, which too often suggests somberness or the clenched jaw.

Difficult subject matter

Some subjects are complicated or abstruse, and are not readily committed to paper. "I've read this report three times and still don't understand it," a production manager complains about a memo from the engineering department.

In this case, sketches or other explanatory material to complement the memo, would have made a difference.

Overcommunication

Readers with an eye for irony had occasion to chuckle at a recent *New York Times* headline: "Anti-Memo Drive." The item then went on to explain that the head of a large advertising agency had succeeded in cutting down on memo writing in his company. How? By eliminating the account executive and assistant account executive—an entire organizational echelon.

That would certainly do it! But the point of relevance here is the implication that memos are a kind of blight on the communications map. And it must certainly be granted that unnecessary memos, like unnecessary phone calls and meetings, are a drain on everyone concerned.

Memos that shouldn't be written in the first place, or copies of memos sent to people who really aren't logical recipients, are a major reason for intracompany communications logjams. Several typical situations tend to stimulate excessive memo exchange:

a. The tendency to "copy in" everybody. It's easier to tell a secretary, "Send that to the entire staff," than to take the time to think through the question of who should receive it. But that's time poorly saved.

b. Fear that someone will be offended by being skipped over. It's an understandable feeling, but it's likely that just as much upset and irritation can be caused by sending out messages to people who have no interest in them.

c. "Here's a great thing I'm doing." An executtive may want to publicize a bit of business that makes him look good. Trouble is, such publicity efforts tend to be quite transparent. The rule still stands: overcommunication can be as bad as undercommunication, and is usually more obvious.

STREAMLINING YOUR COMMUNICATIONS LOAD

Snowblindness, as excessive paper work is sometimes called, is an evil to be fought vigorously. Memos that serve no purpose waste time at both the sending and receiving end. That is why managers from time to time send a message to the source of a memo being circulated by routing slip saying, "Please remove my name from this list." And that's why the memo sender who asks himself, Is this memo necessary? and doesn't send the message if the answer is No, is improving his communications performance.

The two tools that follow can help you streamline your memo load, both incoming and outgoing.

MEMO-USAGE ANALYZER   Chart I. Sending

Name of Communi-cation	To Whom Sent?	About What?	Frequency (how often sent)?	Apply *all* questions to *each* item in the first column. Every *No* answer calls for action.		
					Yes	**No**
(Example) Attendance Report	Mr. Smith, head of Personnel	Department Attendance	Weekly	1. Is the communication really needed (that is, used) by the person receiving it?	☐	☐
				2. If it's a request for information, are you sending it to the best source?	☐	☐
				3. Does the communication ask for information already on hand in another form? (For example, payroll records may serve as an attendance record.)	☐	☐
				4. Are you communicating too frequently about the same things? (A monthly report substituted for a weekly one may cut the job by 75 percent.)	☐	☐
				5. Are your communications frequent enough?	☐	☐
				6. Are you using the best method of communicating for this material?	☐	☐

Notes: ....
....
....
....
....
....
....
....
....
....
....
....
....
....

MEMO-USAGE ANALYZER Chart II. Receiving

Name of Communi-cation	From Whom?	About What?	Frequency (how often received)?	Apply *all* questions to *each* item in the first column. Every *No* answer calls for action.	Yes	No
(Example) Expense Report	Accounting Department	Department Expenses	Monthly	1. Do you really need this communi-cation (that is, do you *use* the infor-mation it contains)?	☐	☐
				2. Does it get to you on time (when it's scheduled to)?	☐	☐
				3. In time? (Getting to you "on time" may still not be in time to do you any good.)	☐	☐
				4. Does it contain *all* the information you need?	☐	☐
				5. Do you need all the information it contains? (If not, you can take a load off the other fellow.)	☐	☐
				6. Does everyone who needs some or all of the information receive it?	☐	☐
				7. Should *you* be passing along some of the information it contains?	☐	☐
				8. Are you getting this communica-tion in the best possible form for your needs? (For instance, you can't file a phone call for record-keeping.)	☐	☐
				Notes:		

Section 6

copies to . . . or, who gets the copies?

It seems like ancient history: At one time there was a physical limit on the number of copies of a memo that could be produced.

B.C.—that is, Before Copiers—determined typists performed by inserting carbon sheets between onionskin paper. Some machines could make more clear copies than others; but as a rule, once you got past six, each additional copy got fainter.

Those last faint copies became an important factor in company life and communication. They were a source of irritation and frustration, hovering as they did between legibility and mystery. But they were also a status factor: the person getting an indecipherable copy knew he was low man on the totem pole.

The advent of the copier changed all that. Now, occasionally, a typist will make one or two carbon copies, just to save herself a walk to the copying machine. But with machine-made copies, the last is exactly the same as the first. Gone is the annoyance and chagrin of the old illegibles. But other aspects of the "copies to" question remain.

MAKING THE CHOICE

A secretary asks, "Who gets copies of this memo?" Sometimes there's a simple answer: for an announcement of a routine staff meeting, copies go to each attendee.

But in some situations, who gets copies—and, just as important, who doesn't—can be a far-from-routine matter:

Sales Manager Paul Harmon is setting out on a swing through New England to call on some key customers. He sends out a memo announcing the visit, providing times and places of each leg of the trip. Included in the "copies to" list are all division managers, because some of them may have some customer-related matters they'd like Harmon to take up during his visits.

But Harmon gets unexpected complaints from others who feel they should have been informed of the trip. Getting a copy of the memo would have been the simplest way to convey this information. The complainers:

• Harmon's boss, vice-president of marketing, who tells him in a belated phone call, "Paul, we should have taken advantage of this trip to have you touch base with some key salesmen. They badly need some personal contact with home office people."

35

• The credit manager, who tells Harmon after he comes back, "We've got a sticky arrears problem with one of the firms you visited. You should have tried to clear it up while you were there."

It's not always easy to select the less obvious copy-to candidates. Harmon's failure to inform his boss was a clear oversight. But the credit manager's complaint was not as predictable. Three moves can help:

• Ask yourself, "Aside from those directly involved, who has some interest, stake, question, connection, with the subject matter of the memo?" (Who has a "need to know"?)

• Ask your secretary who *she* thinks should get a copy.

• When in doubt, *include* the person in the copies-to list.

Many executives feel a need to ride herd on "copies-to" to keep it within sensible bounds. Warren Warner tells his secretary, "Let's stop sending Purchasing and Engineering copies of my memos on our progress on that new product line. It will be months before they have to be brought into it." Very sensible.

FROM THE RECIPIENT'S VIEWPOINT

A recent book dramatizes the importance of the "copies" list. (The "Ernie" in question is one Ernie Blossom, young executive trying to make it up to the loftier rungs of the management ladder):

> In the morning mail Ernie finds an important memo: or rather a carbon of a memo. It is from Ernie's boss, Jeremy Condor, to the President of the company. Condor informs the President of an important step he (J. C.) has taken to streamline the processing of computer printouts.
> Ernie smiles with pleasure at J.C.'s sending him a copy of the memo. This could mean that J.C. now includes him among those who should be kept informed. He's really making it. . . .

From Ernie's reaction, one sees the importance that could be attached to either getting, or not getting, on the "copies" list.

SIGNING YOUR NAME

The matter of copies also brings up the question of signature. An original is easily signed or initialed. But when you are making copies there are several choices. Even if the memo form carries the fill-in "From" line, it's generally advisable to initial or sign the message yourself. You accomplish two things: first, you add a personal quality; and second, it suggests that you have read the message in its final form.

Sometimes, especially, when there is to be a large distribution, the executive will sign the original before copying, so that the copies will include the signature. But many executives emphasize the one-to-one aspect of a message by signing each memo copy individually.

Whenever a message is copied, you end up with an original and as many copies as you have requested. In a typical case, the original typed copy should go to the key person on the list—the individual to whom the memo is addressed if there is only one, or the person of highest status if there are several people listed under "To." Other copies go to all those who are to get the message and to your own file.

The copying machine also makes it possible for you to file longhand replies to memos you've received, of which you want a record. And sometimes you want a record of a self-mailer exchange, where the form sent to you may require only a checkoff answer.

NUMBER OF COPIES CAN MAKE A DIFFERENCE

While the question of copies is not the problem it used to be before the days of the copying machine, it is still not a dead issue today. There are three factors to consider:

Cost

The cost of a one-page copy may be only a few cents, but multiplied by a number of copy-happy memo writers it can reach impressive figures. If a memo is to be spread broadly—over a large staff or even the entire employee roster—other methods of making copies may be considered. In one typical company, the rule is that if there are more than seventy-five copies, the job is switched from the copying machine to the duplication unit—in this particular case, multilith printing.

Appearance

A special personal message to a number of people may suggest originals for each recipient. If there are only a few copies, a typist may be asked to make the necessary number individually. Where quantities are large, say over ten, some managers resort to a tape-controlled typewriter which automatically makes individual copies from a punched paper tape.

Timesaving

If you want to get copies of a memo out in a hurry, you will use the fastest method. Here, you may even waive the niceties of an original signature on each copy, simply duplicating from the master. Or, you may dictate five or ten messages and then leave for a meeting. In such a case, a traditional *modus operandi* is to tell your secretary, "Sign my name and add your initials." For example, *Auren Uris per DH.*

"BLIND" COPIES

One practice deserves special mention. A memo writer may want to send a duplicate of the message to one or more people without the knowledge of the primary recipient. For example, an executive issues a directive to a subordinate and, wanting his boss to know the status of the matter, sends him a copy without indicating this fact on the original. There may be a variety of reasons for not wanting the subordinate to know that the Big Boss has been informed of the assignment: it might cause tension, etc.

But in some cases the blind copy has political implications. A recipient of the memo might be unhappy to know others are being informed of the subject matter, for example. The blind-copy procedure can be a political weapon, and the political potential of the memo is given fuller consideration in the next section.

Section 7

politics
of the memo

Wherever power and influence are up for grabs, politics is bound to flourish. It is no surprise, then, that in the highly competitive world of business, politics is no stranger. In most companies, political strategy plays an important role in advancement. Not that "politics" is necessarily a dirty word—it isn't, any more than all pool is dirty pool. But if you're going to play the game at all, it's important to know the difference between fair play and foul.

For example, it is politically wise to put your best foot forward when dealing with superiors. If you are preparing a memo which will be read by your boss's boss, it's good common sense to take pains with the writing, editing, rewriting, and polishing.

Similarly, there is nothing wrong with using your political instincts when presenting or defending a project in which you have an important stake. More than one budding executive has captured top management attention by his ability to present a reasoned, objective analysis of an issue on which others were sharply (and hotheadedly) divided. Political? Perhaps. But certainly not "dirty" politics.

How can you spot the difference? It's not always obvious. The distinction depends upon the *underlying intentions*. A seemingly innocent memo may serve the most devious of purposes. In the hands of the intransigent, a memo is not so much a tool of communication as a weapon of war. And directed against the unwary, it can do considerable damage.

It is important to become familiar with the political potential of the memo, not in order to use it, but in order to *protect yourself* against it. You never know when you will become the recipient (or victim) of a well-disguised powder keg. With self-protection in mind, let's examine some of the devious purposes to which the memo has been put. They range from the innocuous to the deeply Machiavellian; but each, in its own way, requires sophisticated countermeasures.

The copies' list as a pressure tool

Being left off a routing list of key memos may be a danger signal. One advancement-minded vice-president felt "he had gotten the word" when he was omitted from the group that received the president's confidential memo describing the company's new product plans. He took the omission as a clear indication of how he was evaluated in the company and forthwith began to hunt for a job with a brighter future. That may have been an overreaction, but he was taking no chances.

In its simplest aspects, being copied-in can mean being a member of an "in" group; not getting a copy suggests being out of the group.

Accordingly, some executives use the copies list as a sign of favor or disfavor. A newcomer to a company finds himself on the copies list of a powerful vice-president. Although the substance of the messages may not be particularly relevant, the new manager correctly interprets the memos as a bid for his personal allegiance.

A young Turk makes a strong speech in a meeting favoring cooperation with local ecology people. Suddenly he's dropped from the routing list of a top executive who is opposed to cooperation. "He was trying to put me down," says the young manager ruefully, "and he succeeded."

The just-in-case file

One of the more innocent-seeming political maneuvers involves the memo that starts: "Just for the record . . . ." That opener may be a tip-off that the writer has a mind like a chess player. He firmly believes that a good defense is the best offense and he has the patience to build a case of which an attorney would be proud. Thus, the memo may be addressed to you, but the prime target is really the company file. After the offhand disclaimer that it is merely a recapitulation, the memo does indeed go on to recount pretty much what you already know. Certainly seems harmless enough. And it is—at the moment. But its real mission is to sit quietly in a file drawer, as insurance against the day when the writer wants to be able to prove that he was right early on.

The just-in-case approach may use a seemingly offhand comment inserted in a memo on a vaguely related matter. For example, in one instance, the question of whether a household appliance company should start an inexpensive line had moved from purely rational considerations into the area of politics. Executives were taking sides, trying to sway key company members to their point of view, lining up their teams. At this juncture, a vice-president wrote a long memo to his boss about a marketing situation in which he inserted a few paragraphs to the effect that he was opposed to the idea of the company going into the low-priced field:

At the time of reading, these digressive paragraphs might have seemed innocent enough. But in the mind of the writer was the thought that sometime in the future they might strengthen his hand. If, for example, the company undertook the venture into the new line and failed, the writer could then haul the memo out of his files and show that "he had always been opposed to the idea."

A message "for the record" may show that one was right about a prediction, coura-geous in espousing a minority view, astute in analyzing a situation which subsequently developed as predicted, and so on.

Notice that in each of these situations the same messages could be conveyed by the spoken word. But here's where the *show-ability* of the memo makes it effective. It's not merely that a piece of paper can be produced as evidence, but that *words were put on paper*. The spoken word can often be casual, the written word almost invariably suggests conviction, seriousness, commitment. What's more, no one but the writer is inclined to remember an old memo: it can be left to wither away in the files if it backs the wrong horse!

There is a variation of the just-in-case file that, when used creatively, can provide potent ammunition for the executive who wants to be able to point to the record for his own gain—even when the record may not in fact do him the slightest bit of good. But since a fact can sometimes be created out of whole cloth, one sometimes encounters . . .

The "revisionist" historian

In the academic world the emergence of the historian who rewrites the past with the benefit of hindsight is a relatively new phenomenon. In the business world he has long existed. He is a master of the "for-the-record" type of memo, but with his own self-serving twist. In the process of recording what is purported to be a recapitulation of an earlier meeting or conversation, this politically minded executive adds a few second-thought elaborations to his own in-put and may even imply authorship of some of the worthier ideas that were discussed.

Since memory of just who said what at a hectic meeting is bound to be fuzzy, this tactic can be hard to counter. But if you ever suspect that you are the victim of this kind of rip-off you don't have to risk a direct confrontation. Suggest that a secretary be invited to future meetings, or take your own tape recorder along.

Butter knife in the back

If you've got a lot on the ball, sooner or later you may find yourself working for a boss who feels threatened. Not that he'll ever admit it. He'll be more happy to give you every opportunity to work your damnedest—just so long as he can take the credit. When he finds it necessary to comment on your performance up the line, he'll know better than to bad-mouth you. He'll try to accomplish the same end result by a tactic known as "damning with faint praise," while buttering you up in person.

Let's assume, for example, that you've just knocked yourself out solving an insolvable problem and outlining a cost-free solution which is beyond top management's wildest hopes. Your boss, being less than a complete fool, recognizes it for what it is, and "allows" you to draft a report spelling out the details of the plan. He sends it up to his boss—under his own signature, of course—but adds a generous paragraph: "I want to take this occasion to say that Jim Fallguy has been a real help in getting this project on paper."

Result? Top management thinks your boss is being magnanimous in giving you a share of the credit which they're certain he is entitled to. As far as you're concerned this "credit" is worth zilch!

Your options? Shut up and deal, and hope for a stronger hand, or go over his head and risk losing yours, or peddle your ideas elsewhere. Working for an incompetent boss can be a shortcut to frustration if you want the credit you deserve.

The copy as prime objective

Sometimes the recipient of a memo is merely a sort of straight man. Or, to switch figures of speech, he's the backboard off which the copies—and the message—can be bounced to the *real* target. If you receive a memo that seems to have no purpose, look at the "cc" list. If the sender is an "I'm-gonna-tell-the-teacher" kind of guy, you can be certain that's what he's up to.

Herb Meek was upset when he discovered that Bert Sharp, a competitive colleague, was preparing a promotion campaign stressing the energy-saving features of the Acme Company's clip-on battery-operated night-light. He brought the subject up with Bert, complaining that it was inconsistent with the company's overall advertising slant. Bert listened politely and saw no reason to explain that the matter had been discussed at the highest level and had been enthusiastically received.

Now Herb was not only opposed to the promotion, he wasn't crazy about Bert Sharp either. So he went back to his office just two doors down the hall and dictated a memo to Bert repeating all the arguments he had delivered personally. When Bert received the memo in the interoffice mail, he thought Herb had suffered a bad memory lapse—until he noticed the "cc's" at the bottom of the page. Every important up-the-line executive connected with sales and marketing, up to and including the president of the company, had been included.

Bert was in a quandary. He was smart enough to know that in a political game, the best defense is usually caution. Yet there are times when it becomes necessary to fight fire with fire. And that's what Bert Sharp finally decided to do.

He couldn't afford to risk the possibility that someone getting Herb's memo might decide to reopen the whole idea of the campaign, delaying the project needlessly. On the other hand, he didn't want to go full steam ahead and run into a wall. So he picked up Herb's memo and went around to see his boss, counting on getting to him before he found that carbon in his in-box.

"Say, Dick," he said, "what do you want to do about this love letter from Herb?" Naturally, Dick had to ask, "What love letter?" which gave Bert the chance to tell the whole story, in his own words and with his own interpretation. Needless to say, by the time the carbon was unearthed from Dick's interoffice mail, it had lost its barb, and Bert was free to pursue his project, confident that his boss would back him up if anyone else raised a question.

Notice that the game was won in this case without a direct exchange between the "To" and "From" parties. That's a point worth remembering. The fact is that the political gambit is often more effectively handled "off the record" than in writing. Why let the politician lure you into his game? Far better to cut him off at the bridge—and even after the smoke settles, he won't know what hit him.

Other people's memos

The alert memo-politician is also aware that other people's memos can sometimes be used to good effect. Here are two possibilities:

FLATTERY.   You have written to Bill Hall, one of your subordinates, clarifying a department policy—let's say the subject is the relative priorities your department should give to service demands by Engineering as opposed to Sales.

Bill Hall meets you in the corridor and says, "Boss, that memo was a helluva good statement. Do you mind if I circulate it to other staff members? It would be helpful all around."

You think it's a good idea and agree. Next day your memo is being circulated with a *covering memo* from Bill Hall which reads: "Dear Colleagues: Here is a memo from JB that clarifies a tough nut we've all had difficulty with. I hope it's as helpful to you as it has been to me."

You notice somewhat wryly that Bill Hall has worked a slick ploy. True, what he has done has been helpful and constructive. But in circulating your memo, he has done pretty well for himself. First, he has given the impression that you and he have a close relationship—status point 1. And, he has put himself in the position of addressing his colleagues in a managerial, even condescending, way—status point 2.

Of course, what Bill Hall did is perfectly legitimate. But it's important for an executive to calculate the consequences of having his memos circulated by others, to decide whether the benefits to *him* make it okay to have a subordinate win a little also. And not to be overlooked is the likelihood of a bit of apple-polishing to which you're being subjected. It's okay if you don't mind.

Another version of the same approach has a superior circulating a memo sent him by a subordinate. Here is an example circulated by an executive in a management-consulting firm:

> I would like to pass on a recommendation from Jane Henley to those who may not have read WORKING by Studs Terkel. Jane says that regardless of what you may think about the book's message on the subject of alienation and meaningful work, it can be valuable to us because of the realistic description of work attitudes of a large cross-section of people.

Here the boss is publicizing a subordinate's memo, in a way that makes her look good—in this case making for both effective politics and good management.

AS A TORPEDO.   By using other people's memos in a way that seems similar to a "praise and flattery" objective, it's possible to get a derogatory effect. Using memos as a weapon in this way is more subtle and chancy. The memo-politician has to judge the sophistication of the people he's dealing with:

Don Dale has gotten a high-sounding self-serving memo from a colleague. Annoyed by this obvious attempt to impress him, Don decides to get revenge. He sends a copy of the offensive memo to his boss with a note that says, "Thought you'd be interested in a memo Ken White sent me on the handling of slow collections. Do you think we ought to include this on the agenda of our next meeting?"

Notice that Don Dale's note is cleverly ambiguous on exactly what is to be put on the agenda: the subject of the offending memo, or the ideas of his annoying colleague. But knowing his boss as he does, he's pretty sure that he's not doing his colleague any good—which is the way he wants it.

Kind language

The experienced memoist tends to write tactfully in touching on certain sensitive situations. This consideration may be seen as diplomacy rather than politics. But it deserves mention here because it has political implications and application: One can use tactful language to protect a friend or deal wisely with a foe.

The language we are talking about is a euphemistic way of expression, a way of hiding the seamy side of things—if that seems desirable, and it often does. Here is an example:

A secretary who hasn't been getting along well with her boss is leaving for another job. She writes him a memo that will give him no reason to blame himself for her departure:

Dear Mr._____

I have just been offered a position which includes special writing assignments, increased responsibility and a chance to advance to a managerial job.

I hope you will understand my eagerness to accept this challenge. Accordingly, I will expect to be leaving in two weeks. Please be assured I'll do my part during this period to break in your new secretary, to the best of my ability.

Here are some other common usages:

"I have been asked by our President, Mr. Tom Cowley . . ." Tom Cowley has ordered.

"Paul Barba has resigned . . ." Paul Barba has been fired.

"You are invited to attend . . ." It's a command you'd better heed.

"My assistant _____ has requested a two-month leave of absence to give him an opportunity to recoup his health . . ." An employee with a severe alcohol problem is being given a chance to resolve his difficulty.

Ordinarily, openness and honesty are virtues in communication. But in some touchy and even explosive situations, it can be the height of constructive politics to use indirection and the euphemistic phrase.

Politics as a waiting game

It's worth noting that the politician is usually long on brass but short on patience. If there's one thing he has trouble handling it's uncertainty. That's why the silent treatment is so often the most effective. Ignoring his attack is the most frustrating thing you can do to him. Leave him up in the air long enough and he'll shoot himself down trying to score.

Meanwhile, while you're waiting for that happy ending, what can you do? For one thing, keep your eyes and ears open. Careful observation of the most skillful politician over a period of time will reveal a *pattern*. Once you get the hang of his style you'll have no trouble calling his shots. After that, he's harmless so far as you are concerned. When the waiting gets tough, you can always stick pins in a doll. But whatever you do, don't be too quick to put thoughts on paper—particularly those that lock you into a point of view, or pin you down to a risky action. For further advice on when *not* to write a memo, see the next section.

Section 8

when not to
write a memo

Usually, there's no problem about when to write a memo. You want some information, you answer a question, and so on. But there are times when memos should *not* be written because of unpleasant consequences: You might lose face because of a memo written in the heat of anger; you might take a stand based on incomplete information; you needlessly put yourself on record in a controversial matter.

Here's a rundown of the situations in which the manager should sit on his hands until his memo-writing impulse disappears (of course, you can *write* it, just don't *send* it):

When they are setting you up

"A colleague sent me a query asking for my thinking on our new sales presentation. He knew I had negative views, and wanted me to put them on paper. I wasn't sure how he'd use my memo, but I knew it wouldn't be helping me any. I conveniently 'lost' his request. After a second attempt, which I countered by saying I'd be glad to 'share my thinking when I could get around to it,' he gave up. I never regretted not writing that memo. I know I'd have regretted writing it."

When passions muddy the mind

"If I'd written my boss about what I *really* thought of his hiring a man for a job that I wanted, I'd have been through with this company," confesses a new company president. "I was burnt up by what I considered an injustice. But soon I found myself working with the new man. We proved to be a terrific two-man team—and I soon sent my boss a memo to that effect. A few years later I was made vice-president, and just recently president, of the firm. And my 'rival' is now my general manager—a terrific asset."

When one is angry, scared, hurt—in short, suffering from any of the negative emotions —interoffice communications on the upsetting subject should be postponed. It is inevitable that one's thinking is being influenced, and that afterward, when emotional balance stabilizes, the message will be different. And that usually means better.

When you have nothing to say

Sometimes this is a matter of quantity. It may be okay to write a brief say-nothing memo. But occasionally a gremlin takes over and the executive finds himself turning out page after page of nonsense, when a one-sentence rejoinder would do.

"Our president asked the heads of operating departments, of which I am one, to send along ideas for new products," says a production manager. "I dictated a five-page memo summing up a number of third-rate ideas, and even as I was dictating it I knew it was a lot of hooey. Fortunately, I tore up the memo after it was transcribed, and simply sent a note saying I would give the matter some thought. The following week I had a really good idea, and sent that along. It started a whole new profitable line for us."

To paraphrase a great truth related to another medium, "The absence of memos can be golden."

When face-to-face is better

"My boss asked me to send him my reactions to a lengthy report. Ordinarily, there'd have been no problem. But I hesitated because I wasn't clear on a number of points, including the basic purpose of the report. So instead of writing, I called and suggested that we discuss the matter over the lunch table. It made all the difference. He was able to clarify some key aspects. I understood what he was driving at, and in the exchange I was able to make some useful suggestions. None of that would have been possible without the advantage of the give-and-take conversation."

In addition to the situations already described, there are others that do not suggest complete suspension of the memo-writing impulse, but *do* suggest either hesitation or some other modification of memo-writing procedures:

When there are duties of greater priority

"Recently I spent an hour taking care of interoffice correspondence, while urgent matters were held up. Why? I guess it was easier to talk into a dictating machine than to face up to a tough supply problem," admits an executive.

Putting a high-priority task aside for one of low priority is ill-advised at any time. While the joys of memo writing can be attractive, especially for those executives who like to work with words, first things still should come first.

When your secretary can do it

There are many memos that one's assistant can handle. For the executive to get involved with these is a waste of time. For the routine message, the executive's great contribution should simply be signing it. (But see the caveats on page 29).

When the timing is wrong

There may be nothing wrong with the communication to be sent. However, there may be something in the situation that makes for poor timing.

Manager Bill Tompkins comes in to work one morning and has a difficult time getting his car placed in the company parking lot. He rushes into his office and gets off a big blast to the personnel director asserting that the new parking rules that have just been put into operation are "useless, stupid, unacceptable, ill-advised," and so on. He shortly gets a response saying, "Dear Bill: Still too early to tell." And sure enough, in a few days, the new arrangement works out well. Understandably, this leaves Bill Tompkins feeling like the rear end of a common domesticated animal.

There is another kind of memo that is unwise to write. It's not the timing that sours it, but a basic misdirection. For example:

When it's an unwarranted broadside

A broadside blast may be good for the unloading of the chest, but it's likely to be ineffectual criticism:

In a large insurance company that maintains an employee cafeteria, department head Phil Gerard notices with extreme irritation that some of his supervisors (three out of fourteen) frequently take more than the allotted hour for lunch. He writes a memo to all supervisors that the one-hour lunch maximum must be observed, that punctuality will figure in the annual appraisal and salary review, and so on.

The evils of this shotgun approach are obvious. It unfairly condemns the innocent along with the guilty. The result is that the innocent are offended, while the guilty conclude that everyone else has been committing the same offense they have. Thus, they may feel they can continue what they have been doing without too much danger.

The memo sent in this case is a departure from sound management practice. Gerard made no effort to analyze the problem, determine its causes, and deal just with those. His memo *will* get a result—a lot of his supervisors will be annoyed with him for some time to come.

The interoffice memo is a literary medium of power and subtlety that can accomplish many things. But mastery requires the ability to interpret as well as to create, to discriminate as well as to act. As shown, *not* writing a memo can be a master stroke. That's why many a memo reposing in executive files marked "Not sent" represents a triumph of memo-writing judgment.

And perhaps this section explains why your own memos don't always get answered or an expected message never arrives.

Section 9

writing the long report

There is an effective way to sharpen one's writing skills—not by methods taught in school, which are usually poor, but through techniques used by the professional writer. This path is outlined here, together with the art of editing, which is a special secret of the professionals.

The professional's techniques can of course be used for any piece of writing. But it is especially helpful for longer memos—which often are the important ones.

The simple note written to convey a simple fact—"See you at noon to discuss inventory procedure"—or ask a question—"What's the best time to start processing the Acme order?"—is within the writing skills of everyone. But what we're addressing ourselves to here are those communications which ordinarily might be troublesome because of length or complexity. The task is more manageable when it is broken down into its three major steps: preparation, writing, editing.

PREPARATION

It's a great temptation to plunge right in and try to write the entire piece at one sitting. Don't!

Of course, there are occasional whizbangs who can mull over a problem, summon their secretaries, and dictate a twenty-six-page, single-spaced memo that is a gem of logic and effective prose. But even the gifted people follow certain basic rules. The difference is that they perform these steps mentally with great speed.

Most of us must proceed more judiciously. That means considering key questions:

"What's it about?"

The precise subject must be clear in one's mind. For example, you want to write to your boss about the maintenance problem in your department. Accordingly, remarks about the company picnic or some second thoughts on the production meeting the day before don't belong—not in this memo. Usually, it's wise to confine the message to a single topic, instead of creating a grab bag of varied content.

In addition, to make the writing job simpler and to heighten impact, professional writers do what they call "sharpening the focus" of a subject. Let's say a manager wants

51

to communicate with the head of personnel about absenteeism. If the subject is "Absenteeism," he is out in a vast limitless ocean of facts and figures. But, if the subject is confined to "Absenteeism in the assembly department," that cuts the job down to practical size. Then if the manager wants to sharpen the focus further, his subject becomes "Absenteeism in the assembly department for the first six months of the year." The subject is even more clear-cut.

"What shall I include?"

On every subject of human importance, there's an inexhaustible supply of facts. So you have to draw a line. If too much is included, the reader is bored or drowned in information. If there's too little, he's mystified or confused.

Before one can tell what facts to include, the writer needs a clear image of his audience and their knowledge of the subject. In this respect, your job is easier than the professional writer's. He addresses himself to a huge, unseen audience. But *you* are writing to one person, or just a handful of people: your boss, your fellow-manager, an employee—whoever it is, *you* have a fairly definite picture of what he **is** like in terms of his interests, the pressures on him, his past connection with the subject matter, his objectives in relation to the subject.

Just by way of experiment, consider this problem:

You are the supervisor of a typing pool. You read about a new kind of copyholder in an office-methods magazine and want to buy one. Imagine that you are about to write to your superior asking him to okay the expenditure. Examine each of these four items:

HIS INTERESTS. Is he bored by any discussion of detailed departmental operations? Does he have any special concern about the particular operation involved in the equipment you're discussing?

THE PRESSURES ON HIM. Compared with the other matters demanding his attention, will this look unimportant to him?

HIS PAST CONNECTION. Does he have experience in such matters so that you can afford to omit many details?

HIS OBJECTIVES. What does he want from your department and how do his objectives relate to your proposition? Is he interested in greater volume of work, or is he out to cut costs? Is he concerned about quality performance, or is he looking these days into employee attitudes?

Once you have answered these and related questions, your thinking begins to gel. Now you have a standard against which to choose and reject ideas.

The content

So far, all that's been involved is sitting and thinking. Now you reach for paper and pencil. You begin to make notes—to list ideas.

Most people prefer to put down ideas in brief phrases.

For example, here is a list of ideas prepared by the manager of an insurance company's records department who was proposing changes in filing procedures to his superior:

1. Relieve bottleneck
2. Overtime averages 30 hours per month
3. Employees griping about last-minute notice of overtime
4. Will cut costs
5. Better filing needed
6. Will cut down on misfiles
7. Will talk it over with superior
8. Suited to our operation
9. Absenteeism also caused work problems
10. Got ideas from a case history in a management publication
11. Last year's troubles with filing
12. Minimize errors
13. Will provide more aisle space
14. Expenditure would pay for itself quickly
15. Better service to other departments
16. Easier to teach to new employees
17. Send "old file" cabinets to storage

Some people feel their thinking is crisper if each idea is stated as a complete sentence. There is no universal best way. Whether you should use whole sentences or just phrases depends on your own feelings. Experiment with each; see which seems better.

Test for completeness

How can you be sure you have listed all the relevant items? The journalist has a set of questions that helps prevent oversights:

• **WHO?**   Be clear about the people involved in the situation you are discussing. *Who* is affected—your boss, other executives, fellow managers, employees, customers, suppliers? *Who* caused it? *Who* should be consulted? *Who* can add information?

• **WHAT?**   Here you consider the specific facts of what happened or will happen—conditions, circumstances, events. For example: "The department has been handling three times as much work as last year; we have not added more employees and do not intend to; we are planning to introduce the following changes. . . ."

• **WHY?**   Here you deal with explanations. The key word is *because:* "The accident occurred because . . ." The answer to *why* will show the relationship between things, spelling out cause and effect.

• **WHERE?**   It may be important to discuss where the situation happened or will happen. For example, a proposal for a change might be rejected if the reader thought the idea applied to the whole company instead of just one department.

• **WHEN?**   This question, unanswered, leads to vagueness, and the feeling that key facts are missing. Failure to refer to the time element might lead to those sad post-mortems that begin with: "But I thought you meant it had already been done." Or: "Why didn't you say we had to decide this week?"

Some writers have added several other questions that they ask about their own subject matter:

• **WHICH?**   They point out that in most situations there are alternatives. "It should always be made clear which of two or more things already mentioned in the memo is being discussed." (That's a good rule in thinking about your material—and in actually writing it.)

• **HOW MUCH?**   Where appropriate, there should never be any doubt left as to *how much* or *how long* or *how many.* To talk quantities insures clarity.

Remember, ask yourself all these questions. From the answers, you still have to pick out what you intend to include. Next important question:

"How do I fit the facts together?"

Every fact in a report or memorandum may be crystal clear. The details may be one hundred percent correct. But the reader may throw up his hands and ask: "What's this all about?"

He will—unless the details are *relevant* and are arranged in a *logical sequence,* easy to understand, easy to follow.

The solution is to outline the communication before writing.

The difference is between going for a rambling walk in the woods and taking a trip by railway. In the first case, you can easily get lost; on the train trip, you are always moving on track toward your destination—and you can always find out where you are.

How to outline

A simple outline can be prepared by systematically examining the points listed in your notes:

• **READ YOUR NOTES TO GET A GENERAL IMPRESSION OF HOW THEY ADD UP.** In doing so, you'll notice that some of them are important, some trivial. Some require lengthy explanation; some need only a sentence or a phrase.

For example, in the list made earlier, *"Last year's troubles with filing"* may require three paragraphs, while *"Got ideas from a case history in a management publication"* may be just a phrase in a sentence: "I think I can solve this problem by adapting an idea I got from . . ."

• **ASK YOURSELF WHAT THEME, OR SINGLE THREAD, BINDS TOGETHER ALL THE ITEMS IN YOUR NOTES.**   You should be able to express that all-inclusive idea in one sentence. In the case discussed earlier, the unifying sentence might be:

> I propose a revision of our filing procedures to step up efficiency, cut costs, and improve operations.

The value of a brief statement telling the whole story is that it gives you—as well as the reader—a guide. You can match up each point against two tests:

1. Should the point be included—is it germane to your central theme? In our example, the item, *"absenteeism also caused work problems,"* may be related to the subject of overall efficiency, but it is not relevant to a discussion of a new filing method. You'd cross it off your list. Similarly, you find that *"will cut down on misfiles"* repeats *"minimize errors."* You could then eliminate one or the other.

2. Is the point important to your subject, or only remotely connected? This helps you decide where it belongs in your outline and how much space it should get in your writing.

• **REARRANGE THE INDIVIDUAL ITEMS, PUTTING TOGETHER THOSE THAT LOG-ICALLY RELATE TO EACH OTHER.** This may sound difficult if you've never tried it before. What you do is look for a *common heading* for each group of ideas that belong together.

For instance, in going over the list of ideas, you'll notice that the items fall together under headings like these: the proposal; the conditions it would correct; the feasibility of the proposal; the next steps.

Of course, different people will see different headings and will word them differently. In any case, you now arrange the individual items under the headings that seem logical to you.

You have to handle them separately to make for easier understanding. The philosopher Schopenhauer, whose mind could grasp many complicated abstract ideas, said: "Good writing should be governed by the rule that a man can think only one thing clearly at a time; and, therefore, that he should not be expected to think two or even more things in one and the same moment."

So the rule is: *One thought at a time.*

But in what sequence? Under one heading you may have, say, four ideas. Which should come first? One basic consideration must be kept in mind: *Arrange the individual points in the order which your reader will find easiest to grasp.* Ask yourself: "If I didn't know what this was about, what would I have to know first? Then what? Then what next?" Here's an outline of the file project as developed by using this approach.

A Sample Outline

    I. The Proposal
        Send old file cabinets to storage
        Got idea from case history
   II. The Conditions It Would Correct
        Better filing needed
        Relieve bottleneck
        Overtime 30 hours per month
        Employees griping about last-minute notice of overtime
        Will cut down on misfiles
        Last year's troubles
        Will provide more aisle space

III. Feasibility of the Proposal
    Suited to our operation
    Expenditure would pay for itself
    Better service to other departments
    Easier to teach to new employees
IV. The Next Steps to Be Taken
    Would like to talk it over with superior.

Introduction and conclusion

You have outlined the *body* of your communication. But one more step remains. You need an introduction at the beginning, a conclusion at the end.

Just as the chairman of a meeting cannot introduce a speaker without knowing who he is and what he is going to talk about, you can't choose an introduction without knowing your content. So don't plan your *introduction* until you've outlined the *body*.

For your introduction, pick out what you believe will be most effective in seizing and holding the interest of the person you are addressing. In our sample case, the most likely attention-getter is *"will cut costs."* Of course, this is in addition to a title, or statement of purpose, that immediately tells what the report is about. (See theme statement under How to Outline.)

And what about a conclusion? There are several possibilities. In lengthy reports, the most frequently used conclusion—because it is very effective—is to summarize the main points. For example:

"I hope you will agree that my proposal to change our filing method will correct some current problems. In my judgment, it will surely cut operating costs. If you are interested, let me know when we can get together to talk it over."

Most desirable is an *action* ending: "I suggest an immediate test of the idea"; or, "We could check this new material by placing a sample order."

WRITING

The actual business of getting your piece down on paper may turn out to be the easiest of the three major steps. Here's where many professionals use an approach that solves the problem for them, but leaves amateurs hung up. The professional doesn't worry about the so-called "rules of good writing," or grammar, at this stage. You can emulate the pros in this way:

No matter what problems you have in finding the right words for a particular thought, or in clarifying a particular idea—*don't let anything stop you.* Bull through to the end. You may even have to put down words that you know aren't right or ideas that can't be improved. Regardless of the flaws, push on to the end!

The reason for this move is simple. Once you have a completed draft on paper, you have something to work with. You can improve a word, clarify an idea, and so on. But it's got to be down on paper first.

Two basic rules will help keep you on track in producing your first draft:

Stick to your outline

Go down your list of items and elaborate on each one. This is almost a mechanical process, like filling in the colors on a predrawn canvas. As you write your draft, your mind will be too busy for you to be concerned about the rules of good writing. You'll get to those later. For now, just concentrate on expressing point by point the items in your outline.

Stick to the facts

This doesn't mean you have to leave them "bare." Unfortunately, bare facts don't always communicate. You have to dress them up so that your meaning comes through in the way you want it. For example, in order for a fact to be understood, you may have to explain why: "Everyone must report to Personnel at nine o'clock Monday morning" is a bare fact that might frighten half your people to death. But when you add *why:* "to get your permanent parking space assignments," the information is reduced to realistic proportions.

Push on. Skip points you can't put into words, come back to them later. But finish!

Now comes the third and final step. It further clarifies why you must complete your draft, because once you have it down on paper you can go on to the important phase of:

EDITING

Now you are ready to turn your rough draft into a finished product. This is the professional writer's way. And it's a process that may almost be called secret, it's so little known to nonprofessionals. As a matter of fact, the nonpro thinks that the skill of writing lies in having such a great command of language that you start with the first sentence, go chugging flamboyantly along to the end, without a pause, and end up with a finished piece.

The opposite is true. The very best writers—like De Maupassant, Tolstoy, Hemingway, and Faulkner—would do a second, third, and fourth draft before they were satisfied. "I'm not a writer, I'm a rewriter," says one author with many books to his credit.

To start your rewrite, you change your viewpoint. Now you assume the role of the reader instead of the author. You are about to pass judgment on *what you have actually said,* and you don't want to be confused by any recollection of *what you intended to say.*

First read it for the overall effect. If you run into a point that is unclear or badly worded, don't stop to change it—just put a mark in the margin. Similarly, if something is omitted, note it briefly on the side, and then go right on reading your draft.

When you have finished the whole text, go back and work on the details. Here are some suggestions on what to look for:

Review your introduction

In outlining your material, you started with an item that you hoped would seize and hold the interest of your reader. In rereading the beginning, ask yourself these questions:
• **WHERE DID YOU TELL YOUR READER EXACTLY WHAT YOUR SUBJECT IS?**
The earlier, the better! As a general rule, people don't want to be left in the dark and they resent the person who does it to them.
• **WHERE DID YOU TELL YOUR READER HOW IMPORTANT THE SUBJECT IS?**
Again, the earlier the better. Notice, too, that "important" can mean different things. Important to him? to the company? to you? to others?

Work on words and phrases

As you read, you'll find a word that doesn't sound right. Too strong, or too weak. Not clear enough. Not really what you had in mind. Not sufficiently arresting. Change these. Eliminate unnecessary verbiage (called "cutting" by the writing pros). Eliminate a statement you feel is inadequate. Correct the grammar.

Search for repetitions

But don't assume that repetition must automatically be eliminated. Sometimes there is a good reason for repeating yourself. But if you are doing so, be sure you know why:
FOR EMPHASIS.   To make an important point stand out, you may be perfectly justified in repeating. Only, be sure it really is important.
FOR CLARITY.   You may want to repeat an old point in a new context in order to make sure your reader will understand. You can't risk the possibility that he has forgotten the point, or that he may fail to make the connection. So it may be wise to do your reader the courtesy of saying, "As I pointed out before . . ." But if you find too many "as I mentioned earlier's," it may signal the need for reorganization.

One word is better than two

Extra words are excess baggage. In business especially, it's best to "travel light." When you read over your first draft, concentrate on eliminating heavy phrases. Here are some of the worst offenders:

Heavy	Light
accompanied by	with
afford an opportunity	allow
at all times	always
at this point in time	now
due to the fact that	because
experience has indicated that	we learned
in the near future	soon
in regard to	about
meets with our approval	we approve
prior to	before
subsequent to	after

Here's how one manager was able to edit a paragraph in a memo. First version:

> Please afford my secretary an opportunity to check the Jones file. Since you at all times have cooperated with such requests, I hope you will acquiesce once more. Due to the fact that this information must be forthcoming in the near future, I trust you will be able to grant permission at your earliest convenience.

Here's a streamlined version:

> Do you mind letting my secretary check the Jones file? We need some information urgently and your help would be greatly appreciated.

If you think the first version of the two paragraphs above is exaggerated, of course, you're right. But the sad fact is that it is representative of much business writing, even today.

Look for omissions

Are there any vital points that you have omitted? The test is whether you have left out anything that the reader needs to know.

Omissions usually occur because the writer is so steeped in his material that he assumes everybody else knows the details.

Among the most common errors in this respect are:

• failure to identify people mentioned
• failure to include definitions of unfamiliar terms that are used
• failure to describe equipment or procedures involved in the situations under discussion.

For a fuller checklist, see the cues on *What, When, Where,* etc., described on pages 53 and 54.

Apply the relevancy test

In rereading, one of your primary objectives should be to cut out as much material as you can. But how can you decide what to drop?

Here, your test is to go back to the summary sentence you used in planning your outline. If in doubt about any item, simply ask yourself: "Is this necessary in order to convey my basic idea?"

Remember that many things you might include in conversation have no place in a written report:

"I was talking about this with John—I ran into him in the washroom—and I found that we have the same problem of untrained help." Compare that with the speed and ease of understanding in: "John and I both have the same problem of untrained help."

Check the flow of ideas

This point can best be understood if you examine the following memo. We have numbered the sentences for easy reference.

(1) We could arrange with Billing for part-time use of their calculating machine. (2) We have a girl who is capable of using the machine. (3) The workload on our present calculator is more than it can handle. (4) The Billing supervisor says it would be OK with her. (5) The overload is not enough to warrant a second machine as yet.

Obviously, in this paragraph one idea does not lead logically to the next. As an exercise in editing, rearrange the sentences by just listing in the margin the numbers in the order you prefer. (Here's a suggested sequence which may not make great literature, but does make an intelligible paragraph: 3, 5, 1, 4, 2.)

In your own writing, you will rarely have to do more than rearrange a few sentences, if you outlined your material in advance.

This check on the sequence of sentences within each paragraph is important. It saves your reader the trouble of having to rearrange your ideas. In many cases, he may not do it—he'll just give up.

Weigh your conclusion

People tend to remember best the last thing they hear or read. Your conclusion makes the final impression.

As you reread it, ask yourself what it accomplishes. Does it nail down your basic point? Keep in mind the main purpose behind your writing. Is it:
- to inform?
- to ask information?

• to produce action?

There are as many purposes as there are motives in human beings. Your conclusion, directly or indirectly, must reflect your purpose.

In judging your final draft you don't have to go it alone. Remember how often books contain an acknowledgment: "and to my wife, who helped in the final preparation and finishing of the manuscript"? Many a writer's wife, children, colleagues, have been asked to read drafts, and so pretest the writing for clarity, interest, impact. So you can get another opinion, if you like, on your writing, as an assist in putting it into final shape. A tried-and-true secretary has few peers for this assignment.

In suggesting the best way to put your thoughts in writing, we have not stressed the usual "rules." Instead, we have emphasized that the secret of good business writing lies in three key steps: outlining your draft before it's written, writing a rough draft, and reviewing it after you've put the words on paper.

The next section describes memo analysis, in which probing actual memos leads to a greater awareness of their problems and opportunities.

Section 10

memo analysis: a self-help tool

There are many ways to improve the quality of your outgoing correspondence. One, certainly, is experience. But even experience is no guarantee unless you are aware of some of the key elements that make for effective writing.

This section describes a method for analyzing memos, such as the ones that cross your own desk, and pinpointing what is *effective* about them as well as what *muddies* the message. With a small investment of time, you can solve some of the crucial problems of memo writing by learning to recognize the more common pitfalls.

Every company has its own counterpart for the memo-happy executive whose out-box is piled mountain-high with correspondence aimed up and down the line. All too frequently, however, he is doing a worse job of "putting himself across" with colleagues than the nonsender. In short, "doing it" isn't enough. It's knowing what you're doing that pays off.

FOUR STEPS TOWARD IMPROVEMENT

There's a wealth of wisdom available right in your own office and you can tap it with this simple four-step experiment. You will be amazed how much you can learn from an analysis of your own daily mail.

Step 1

Gather a sample of interoffice memos you've received recently, or ask your secretary to do it for you. If your correspondence is filed as it comes in, ask your secretary to accumulate the memos that come your way for the next few days. Anywhere from a dozen to twenty pieces of correspondence will do the trick.

Step 2

Reread these memos, dividing them into two piles. In one pile put all the memos that you feel are poorly written—those that for one reason or another you don't like, those that make difficult or dull reading. This is your "NG" pile. Into the second pile go the

63

"OK" memos—those that you feel do the job for which they were intended, and those you would be willing (or glad) to sign your own name to.

Disregard content at this point. You may find, for example, that in one communication the boss has been critical of something you've done. If you can admit, however grudgingly, that his memo is well written, it still goes into the OK pile.

Step 3

Concentrate on the poorly written memos first. Go through the NG pile critically and try to pinpoint the *reasons why* each one "turned you off." You may find that some memos have negative qualities that are easier to identify than others. Verbosity, for example, is easy to spot. But, of course, there are other possible drawbacks besides that of using a dozen words where one word would do. Keep on going through the group of memos and note on a sheet of paper each quality that you find objectionable.

One executive, following this procedure, was able after fifteen minutes of analysis to come up with the following list of undesirable memo characteristics:

• **UNCLEAR PURPOSE:** The item in which this characteristic was observed started off with a rambling discussion of the necessity for cutting costs. After six paragraphs of this, the writer then stated the memo purpose—an idea he had for revising an office procedure.

• **OVERLOAD OF BIG WORDS AND STILTED PHRASES:** "I am of the opinion that it is highly desirable to create an early liaison between sales and production on this vital matter. Ultimate considerations should be taken up," etc.

• **UNATTRACTIVE HARD-TO-READ APPEARANCE:** Two pages of single-spaced typing, with no paragraph breaks or subheadings.

• **NO PURPOSE, BUT AN ULTERIOR MOTIVE:** The memo was really only an expedient for the writer who was expressing his gripes and complaints.

Step 4

Next, proceed through your OK pile and spot the qualities that make for a well-written job. In some cases you may not be able to decide off the cuff exactly why you find a particular memo easy, lucid, effective, reading. You may have to do some thinking about the individual pieces. But stick with it, and eventually identification will come.

Here's one manager's list of attractive and desirable memo qualities:

    Early statement of purpose
    Clear statement of purpose
    Persuasiveness
    Businesslike, to the point
    Easy to read
    Good organization.

COMMON PROBLEMS TO LOOK FOR

If you follow the analysis procedure to this point and draw up your own list of elements that make for effective or ineffective memos, you will have completed more than half the job of developing your own memo-writing formula. But don't be discouraged if you find that it's easier to separate the good from the bad than it is to spot the crucial elements that separate the two. Trust your gut feelings—they are probably right. The following list of common problems can help you translate that gut reaction into constructive analysis:

Early statement of purpose

"Early" doesn't mean in the first sentence (it may), but it should mean in the first paragraph. If you're halfway down page 1 and you're still not certain what the writer is driving at, you were right to put the memo in your NG pile. Try to find the sentence where he really comes to the point. See what would happen if you moved this sentence up to the top.

Clear statement of purpose

This seems like an obvious point, but it's often troublesome. "My department has been having difficulty with deliveries," a manager writes to his boss. And then he goes on with a general discussion of the transportation problems that have hampered his operation off and on over the past year. What's the "purpose" of this memo? Is it merely an information message, to let the boss know about the problem? Is the manager going to suggest holding conferences with the carriers? Or is his idea to change the means of transportation? The "meander" effect of memos often results from this one lapse, failure to make clear the thrust of a message.

A "clear" statement of purpose means a simple and specific statement that will explain why this particular memo is being written at this particular time. Two examples:

"I would like you to okay the extra expense of direct messenger service for small shipments from local suppliers."

"Can we get together at your earliest convenience to discuss this transportation problem?"

Persuasiveness

Frequently a memo is written to get someone to go along with an idea or a course of action. The correspondent may be anyone in or outside the organization.

But the art of being persuasive by means of the written word is somewhat different from talking, and is, of course, a subject all by itself. However, if you feel that one of your sample memos flunked on this score, test it against these two basic requirements:

• **DOES IT MAKE THE GOAL ATTRACTIVE?**   If it didn't sell you on what's in it for *you,* then it certainly missed its mark. Here's one way to sell your reader: "I feel this idea, if properly worked out, could be the solution to a problem that had been a headache to all of us. In your own case, for example, it would mean that you'd be rid of the nuisance of supervising six people by 'remote control.' "

• **DOES IT SUPPORT ALL STATEMENTS OR ARGUMENTS BY FACTS?**   No one is persuaded by rhetoric alone. Analyze your memos for supporting data such as this: "A similar move was made by the ABC Company one year ago. In this twelve-month period the company has achieved the following results . . ."

Businesslike, to the point

Don't confuse this with brevity. You could write a 1,000-page report that would still be businesslike and to the point. This quality can be summed up in a single word: "relevancy." As long as everything in it bears on the basic purpose of the memo, it's on the beam. Any memo that wastes the reader's time, however, belongs in the reject pile.

Easy to read

This quality can be built into a memo in several ways. Here are some things to look for in this regard:

• **LEGIBILITY.**   Of course, the reader should be able to read what you've said. If you send off a handwritten message, write carefully enough for each word to be decipherable. If you are burdened, as so many of us are, with a can't-read script, print (short messages) or use the typewriter. A good space between lines, and sufficiently wide margins are other generosities a recipient will appreciate.

• **INFORMALITY.**   In most cases—except for a serious report—it helps to let the spark of humanity show through. Use the recipient's name within the message, in a conversational matter. Inject, where appropriate, a phrase or sentence that reflects your friendship or past contacts: "The fact is, George, this situation is pretty much like the one we tackled last year at the Chicago meeting, remember?"

• **INTEREST.**   Material can be either inherently stimulating or dull as dishwater. If a person is describing how something happened, for example, he's telling a story that is likely to sustain a reader's interest. The writer is in a less fortunate position, however, if his subject centers on a mass of data. One way to prevent smothering the reader in detail: put the figures, and so on, in a separate section at the end of the message.

• **BREVITY.**   Generally, short words make easier reading than long ones, ditto short sentences, ditto short paragraphs.

Good organization

This quality can pop out at you from the page. A poorly organized memo may look like a solid block of typing. You approach the task of reading it with the resignation of an explorer, machete in hand, confronting a dense jungle.

The well-organized memo, on the other hand, is as attractive as an open, sunny field. The precision and neatness of a well-organized memo are not unlike a neatly fenced countryside. Here are two specific points that make for good organization:

• **TITLE.** Even if the interoffice form doesn't have the printed word "subject" at the top, there's no reason for the writer not to add it.

• **MAIN HEADINGS.** Except for the very brief message, a memo lends itself to division into two or more sections. Here, for example, are four headings used in a memo discussing a grievance case: Background; The Grievance Incident; Developments in the Handling of the Case; Present Situation.

The lives of many executives have been made a lot easier by their secretaries, who have been able to suggest the positioning of headings and subheads in their memos.

CHECKING YOUR PERFORMANCE

The ultimate payoff in analyzing desirable and undesirable characteristics of incoming memos is that you can incorporate the good qualities and avoid the bad in your own memo style. It's an application of the golden rule: you'll be doing unto others what you'd like them to do for you.

The checklist below can help you analyze how much your memo-writing performance is improving:

1. Do people you send memos to often have to check you for:
   a. Additional information (for example, to supplement a report)?
   b. Clarification of a communication you've sent them? (Do they ever say, "I couldn't understand what the message was getting at"?)
2. Do your subordinates complain about the lateness of memos containing key information?
3. In communicating with your superior:
   a. Do your memos tend to arrive "too late to be of help"?
   b. Do you have to telephone to give additional information that should have been included in the memo?
   c. Does he have to contact you for an explanation of your memos?
   d. Do you usually succeed in selling him on a pet idea?
4. In your communications with fellow executives:
   a. Are you sending routine memos that no longer fill a purpose?
   b. Do you know of any change in method of communications that would improve results (for example, switching from memos to conferences)?

Keep in mind that you have available to you a gold mine of information about your memo-writing practices. Just check through copies of the last ten memos you wrote. How do they stack up against the list of "desirable characteristics" you developed by examining the other fellow's correspondence?

A FINAL (EXCITING) THOUGHT

Increasing one's skill in handling the written word is a major aspect of mental growth and in sharpening an essential management skill. Remember, some people have written their way up the ladder. Why shouldn't you add one more worthy name to the list?

part ii

memos for every occasion

The memos in this section come from a number of sources. Every effort has been made to make the collection representative. A sufficient number of samples of each type has been included to illustrate the range and nuances of each.

Many of these memos come from the files of practicing executives. Others come from published sources; for example, the David O. Selznick memos, of particular interest because of the famous movie stars discussed in a business context. Often, writers have requested anonymity. Where this has not been the case, attribution has been made in appropriate fashion. A portion of the samples reflect the author's hand, in rewriting, disguising identifying elements, or in shortening. The effort has been made, in each such case, to enhance the utility of the memo as a model. Both good and bad aspects are pointed out to further sharpen awareness of effective practice.

The samples are divided into categories, to simplify the finding of specific forms as well as to illustrate the many facets of the memo.

Some of the categories tend to overlap. For example: An Acknowledgment memo understandably may include an expression of thanks, qualifying it for the Gratitude heading as well. Such overlaps have been resolved by arranging the memos on the basis of what has been considered the major thrust of each message.

Notice that salutations and complimentary closes have been omitted in the models. This has been done for two reasons: first, to save space, and second, the present-day usage of these two formalities is highly personalized. Often they're omitted altogether, that is, rather than saying "Dear Somebody," the designation "To" is used. And the close is often omitted, although initials or signatures still prevail. But you are free to choose: One president of a large company starts his memos to employees with "Dear Folks." Why not?

USING THE MODELS

The samples may be helpful in a number of ways:

As a direct model

In some cases the wording of a message as given may be sufficiently close to what's needed to be used almost as is. Of course, minimum changes are recommended—in wording, phraseology, etc., so that the memo reflects the writer's personal image and language and satisfies his mood and meaning.

Loose adaptation

The example may be roughly duplicated—in terms of general content, length, and so on. The final version might only vaguely reflect the original model.

Trigger

A given sample may sound a theme, use a word or phrase that provides just enough to start the memo-writing process.

In addition, the models may help you clarify your thinking or feeling. For example, something may have happened that you feel requires the writing of a memo. But what sort of memo should it be? Let's say, a colleague has sent you some material that will prove quite helpful. Skimming the categories of memos, you see the heading, "Ideas," but then you will also see "Proposals." A brief reading will show you which type of message is the more appropriate in the particular situation.

In some cases the model may suggest what you *don't* want to say—which is another way of clarifying your thinking.

It should be clear that this collection can be as helpful to the secretary or executive assistant as to the executive. Assistants to executives, familiar with the sample memos here available, can be of particular help in aiding their bosses with their outgoing correspondence.

index of memo categories

74

sample memos

ACKNOWLEDGMENTS   (*see also* Gratitude)

Incoming mail brings information: a sketch for a new ad from the art department, a report from Nigeria sent by one's boss during his travels. You want to let the sender know the item has been received. Or perhaps it is an act that is to be acknowledged, or an obligation. Additional comments are possible: you want to register a reaction, ask a question, and so on.

This form resulted in one of the shortest memos on record, a response to an engineer's 160-page explanation of a technical point in the design of a piece of food machinery. The message from the vice-president, production: "Gotcha."

Sometimes it can be simple.

Your meeting notes of the personnel seminar arrived in this morning's mail. Thanks.

A bare-bones message like the above is okay for routine acknowledgments. However, sometimes there is more to be said.

The color samples for the new order of acetate molding powder were delivered yesterday. I'll pass them along to Bill Brame after I've finished with them. Bill will let you know the results of the tests.

Sometimes you have to add a qualification: note a missing item, etc.

This is to acknowledge receipt of the record of purchases made by my department for the first quarter. I've made a brief check and find that some purchases made in January are missing. After I've made a more thorough check, I'll let you know of the discrepancies uncovered.

75

A warehouse foreman writes the head of maintenance to acknowledge an obligation.

I know it's a week after the date I promised to have the twenty 50-gallon paint drums removed from the alley next to Building B. On Monday I expect an extra man to get us over the short-handedness, and so the job should be done by Tuesday, latest.

In response to a report from his controller that losses would greatly exceed planned profit, a well-known hotel executive sends an off-beat acknowledgment.

Had he lived, Mr. Lavenson would have acknowledged your memo of June 12. When he read it, he died of shock. Mournfully,
> Ruth Zarick
> Secretary to the late Mr. Lavenson
> Jim Lavenson
> President of The Plaza

It may be desirable to itemize what's been received: to a company librarian.

Once again the library has come through like the marines. So that we both have a record, the books I have received from you are:
Drucker—*Practice of Management*
Mackenzie—*The Time Trap*
Battaglia & Tarrant—*The Corporate Eunuch*
Uris—*Thank God It's Monday*
Thanks for your excellent service. I'll see to it that the Big Boss shows his appreciation for your efforts at budget time (joke).

In response to a congratulatory note from a female employee. Informal breeziness can blow a gale—if the relationship between sender and receiver is appropriate.

Words! Words! Words! How about a date for dinner?

ADMONITION

A subordinate is undertaking a risky course of action; a colleague invades an area that is not his responsibility. One wants to voice concern, to warn, advise, caution, suggest alternatives. Another purpose of the admonitory memo: to put one's views on record, in case later developments raise questions of one's judgment, attitude, or alertness.

Managing editor of a staff-written monthly publication points out a cost leak. The deadpan, authoritarian tone may get obedience, but is not likely to get cooperation. More "we" and less "I" would make the message more persuasive.

The Production Department tells me that author's alterations are consistently running at about two times an acceptable level. I have reviewed the job jackets on our publications and it is clear that the excess AA's result from inadequate attention in preparing copy for the printer.

It is extremely important to do a careful line count and rough dummy before sending copy out. Changes on the galleys should be limited to those necessary for copy fitting. Rewriting, or adding new copy at the galley stage is far too costly.

I hope that we will be able to reduce our AA expenditures by 50% starting next week.

From a division manager to the company's purchasing chief. A few facts and for-instances would have helped make a stronger case.

I understand you're considering placing my order for desks with the XYZ Furniture Company. I have it on good authority that they're an unreliable source. You may not want to take my word for it, but I hope you'll at least check this out before placing the order.

This communication is the caption of a New Yorker *cartoon showing a nighttime cleaning lady picking up a dictating-machine mike and saying, "Memo to the executive director, vice-president, heads of departments and all members of the staff . . ."*

Wipe your feet.

From a sales manager to the head of sales promotion. The writer has done a good job of stating his case, and being quite open about his opposition.

We pretty thoroughly thrashed out the whole question of prize contests in our meeting—I thought. My feeling was that enough negative points were made, highlighting the risks, to kill the idea. But now I hear from J. P. that you're still exploring the scheme, and that you're enthusiastic about the possibilities. Well, you may know something I don't, but after the discussion today, I'm definitely anti-contest. Just want you to know this memo is for the record, and I'm sending a copy to J. P.

This message was posted on company bulletin boards. The message wisely avoids the angry reprimand for wrongdoing, yet makes a strong and reasoned case.

It's been noticed that some employees have been parking in the executive area. This misuse of our available space is causing problems with our overall parking plan.

The new area just completed provides convenient parking for everybody. To the few who are failing to comply: please don't create needless difficulties. Anyone parked improperly from now on will be asked to re-park during the lunch hour.

From one production manager to the head of a neighboring department. Somewhat sharp, but to the point.

Pete Jones tells me you've given him an assignment to do "on the side." Since Pete is in my department, taking such a step without consulting me is most objectionable. I've told him to disregard your request. And, in the future, if you want to take up work matters with my subordinates, please check with me first.

ADVOCACY

From time to time you want to advance a view, align yourself with a cause, advocate a policy or principle. The wording and assertiveness of such statements may be critical: made overly strong, they sound argumentative; too weak, the question arises as to the point of the message.

Or your opinion, point of view, or counsel may be sought on a matter. An effective response calls for a number of elements: a description of the situation or problem; a clear statement of your recommendations; and, finally, the reasons for them, if this seems appropriate.

The writer was sent a query on his opinion of the new reception-room decor. The reply was penciled on the original message.

In favor!

From a staff member to his boss, effectively raising a question. Suggesting a follow-up discussion is a good way to avoid a long one-sided presentation of a controversial view without knowing how it's being received.

An outcry against meetings is popular these days. *Everyone* is supposed to complain that they are a waste of time, etc. Perhaps, in some cases, they are objectionable. But I have come to feel that our group is suffering from *insufficient* contact, and that *more* meetings—specifically, a regular weekly meeting—would serve to end a serious communications gap. Perhaps there's more to be said about this than I could put down on paper now. Could we get together to discuss this further—perhaps at lunch?

Sent to a Harvard-educated personnel manager with a tendency to screen out prospective employees who don't possess the "right school" credentials by a line executive who sees native intelligence and experience at least as valuable as the old school tie. This is a human and persuasive statement on a key policy of personnel selection.

I stand upright for motherhood; I am against sin; I am strongly in favor of two sexes; and, I do believe wholeheartedly in advanced education (even, if necessary, at Harvard!).

BUT—I am dead set against the stilted cliché of either word *or thought* on any important subject—especially, the playing of (safe) averages in measuring people's talent. Those who do will assuredly miss too many *all-important* exceptions that preclude mediocrity in the business world.

My personal thinking favors heavy formal education for high-level competence in the technical professions. But, in business, no amount of books, tutoring, or case studies will an entrepreneur make. Innate shrewdness coupled with school-of-hard-knocks experience cause the workforce and the dollars to behave so that profits pile high. And, after all is said, that particular result is indeed the basic reason for the existence of any business enterprise.

Please, for the mutual benefit of us all—put élitist theory aside for a moment . . . realize that we'll be better than the average or the mediocre only if we act differently from the average or the mediocre.

80

A production manager to head of purchasing. By noting the hostile tone of the memo received, and showing that it's being taken in stride, the writer de-steams the argument. His clear statement of his position and a call for a meeting helps put the issue on a mature level.

Got your pugnacious little note this morning, and it may surprise the hell out of you to know that I agree. I'm all in favor of red tape that helps instead of hinders. I'm even willing to fill out all the forms and requisitions your department provides—for ordinary purposes. But when one of my people calls for special service as a result of a production emergency and the answer he gets suggests that red-tape delays will mean he won't get what's needed until after the time that it will do any good, then I say the procedures are wrong, and should be reshaped to fit needs.

I'd be willing to discuss this matter further in the presence of Bill Golden. When would this be convenient?

A division manager writes to a department head about one of the latter's foremen, who happens to be a minority-group member. Since the writer is the recipient's boss, this message is noteworthy for its objectivity and forbearance. It's calculated to help the department head rethink the problem of his foreman without authoritarian pressuring, and also provides a showpiece for the department head who may at a later date have to defend his decision to continue Foreman Dave Lee in his post despite a poor early record.

I've just seen the latest production and quality reports from the Forming Department, and they show no improvement over last month. This is bad news for Dave Lee, and I've heard some people say the simplest way to improve matters is to replace him. But I'm still a booster, and I'll tell you why:

Six months is too short a period to adequately judge a new foreman.

I've stopped by the Forming Room from time to time and I have the impression that Lee is really trying. And in those visits, I've also come to feel that the people respect him, and now, unlike the beginning, they're pulling with him.

I'm afraid those who say, "Yank Lee," are those who thought he shouldn't get the job in the first place. In other words, theirs isn't a considered judgment but the continuation of an old bias.

Finally, I have to say that removing Lee now would at very best be premature, and the company could be accused of unfair treatment.

As you know, my working relationship with Lee is peripheral. But since you are his direct superior, I thought you'd like to have my opinion.

From a manager to the head of an entertainment committee. This type of after-the-fact summary is a good way to benefit from and make history. While it's doubtful that the receiver will remember to haul out the message during the next Christmas planning session, the sender can put it in his own tickler file and recirculate it at the proper time.

Ed, we both know how the managerial mind works, and that's why I'm sending you this memo now, even though it applies to something a year off.

Thanks to the efforts of you and your committee, we've just had one of the most successful Christmas parties ever. Everyone I talked to had a good time, nothing happened to sour the evening, every detail from the place to the unpretentious entertainment was just right.

Now, what I expect is that encouraged by this year's success, some of the powers that be are going to say, "Next year, let's do it even better—bigger, flashier, and so on." And that's exactly what I'm opposed to. I think it's *because* we had the party in our own recreation room, *because* we used our own entertainment talents, *because* we didn't try to kick a hole in the sky, that things worked out so well.

So keep this memo handy, and next year, when planning starts for the annual get-together, please pull it out and circulate copies to the committee. I just don't want to spoil a good thing.

A division manager explains why he favors a new training program for supervisors. His view has the benefit of being supported by firsthand observation.

You asked for my reaction to the Research Institute of America's "Living Case History" program. Having just witnessed a demonstration of one of the training tapes, there's no question: I'm solidly in favor.

As the meeting progressed, I watched the reactions of the supervisory participants. I've seldom seen such interest and involvement brought out by any training medium. And for me, the clincher was the discussion of the case that followed—lively, relevant, and above all, practical.

If scheduling and other arrangements can be made, I'd be glad to have my supervisors participate in a program built around the RIA material.

AGENDAS

See Meetings, Agendas

AGREEMENT

There are two kinds of agreement:
 • *Acquiescence.* A statement that you see eye to eye with a colleague about a given matter.
 • *A statement of an understanding.* In this case you have "made an agreement" with someone to do something by a given time, for example.
 The samples below represent typical items in both areas.

From the editor in chief to the head of printing production, to get agreement on operating procedures.

Without reference to any particular incident I think it should be understood between us that there should be no changes in the type specified for any publication without the knowledge of the editor responsible for the publication. With the current increase in workflow, I can well understand that some jobs may move forward faster when an editor is bypassed. However, the resetting of eight or ten galleys of unsatisfactory type would be a high price to pay.

A manager suggests to a colleague that they take joint action on a matter about which they are like-minded.

From what you said in the conference this morning, it's clear that your views on the inadequacy of intracompany contacts are pretty much like mine. For example, I think it's just unforgivable that there has been no interdepartmental meeting for two years. Surely we all have a great deal to gain by learning how the other guy is living—or trying to. If you think it's a good idea, why don't we corner T. W. at some early date and drop the proposal in his lap?

To the movie company's treasurer reassuring him that the writer agrees with him on the need for care in spending. As cinema history indicates, GWTW became an all-time great, well worth every penny of expense.

To: Mr. John Wharton   January 13, 1937

Dear John:

I understand you perfectly about *Gone With the Wind.* I am aware that we can spend a lot of money unnecessarily on the picture. On the other hand, it is one picture which, if done perfectly, can almost with certainty return an enormous profit, in my opinion; and which, if cheated on, can cut down these potential profits substantially.

I think, however, I know what you have in mind, and you may be sure that we are not approaching the picture with any foregone conclusion that it has to be enormous in size and has to have an exceptionally high cost, even for big pictures. I myself have no idea what the picture will cost, but as soon as we get close to a first script, I will see if we can arrive at a preliminary budget.

Memo From David O. Selznick

A manager communicates to a colleague at his same level on a matter of company practice, and indicates his agreement with the recipient's views.

Someone from Personnel (here nameless) was complaining to me that it's your cockeyed idea that department heads and foremen should have a greater say in hiring. Well, it's my cockeyed idea that you're perfectly right. I never could see any sense in having Personnel do the final selection in hiring anyone, from a file clerk to a vice-president. The outlook for mischief is pretty strong if a supervisor can push an employee back on Personnel before the probation period is past and say, "He's no good." It's only when the supervisor makes the final selection—of course, Personnel should do the initial screening—that he has the incentive to make the employee fit in successfully.

You have my permission—in fact my full backing—to show this to Mr. Gaines, so that he can take the matter up with Personnel.

A nonbeliever falls into line, and generously admits he's been wrong—with a copy to an up-the-line executive.

I'm a lousy loser, Bill, but after your presentation yesterday, I'll have to withdraw my objection to your plan to centralize the purchasing of office supplies. The facts were too impressive to deny. Notice that I'm sending a copy of this to Albie.

A manager adds his weight to an employee's proposed advancement.

Of course I agree that Helen Bailey could take on the job of assistant. Anyone who told you I think differently is just misinformed. Remember, I hired her originally, and she worked as my secretary for two years, so I have a pretty good idea of her capabilities. I'm willing to add my vote to see that she gets the promotion, if you think it will help.

Sometimes the agreement is qualified. And when it is, the reluctance is best stated, to avoid someone at a later date saying flatly, "But you agreed. . . ."

You ask what I think of your idea to take Ben Boyle out of Production for a while and have him make service calls in the field. To be quite frank, I'm lukewarm, by which I mean there are advantages and disadvantages. And as I see it, they very nearly balance each other. But I'm willing to go along for a single reason, and that is, that essentially what you're talking about is a trial. So give it a whirl for several months. And then let's review.

ANNOUNCEMENTS

(*see also* Hiring; Meetings, Agendas; *and* Policy Announcements)

This is an essential information area. Decisions are made, action taken, jobs changed, projects undertaken, people hired. To avoid misunderstandings and ball-ups, accuracy in detail is essential. The memo may be addressed to one person or to everyone in the company. It may be simple and brief or ring with the resonance of trumpets—if the subject matter is sufficiently noteworthy.

This is one type of message when *omissions* can cause great difficulties or embarrassment: a meeting room adorned only by the chairman, because no one else was informed, a newly hired staff member whose arrival isn't anticipated, are but two examples.

From a division head to his supervisors, announcing a meeting to be chaired by the company president.

Mr. Adams would like to meet with all supervisors on Monday, December 10, at 11:00 A.M. in the conference room. My understanding is that he would like to discuss the significance of the energy and other shortages for the company and on the work we do.

A personnel director calls a change of signals for a supervisory meeting. A light touch adds spriteliness to a routine message.

For all those who love procrastination, here's good news—the management meeting on handling absenteeism has been postponed from Friday, Feb. 1, to Friday, Feb. 8. More thinking time, folks!

A common form of the "To All Employees" message.

The office will close at 3:00 P.M. on December 24, to help you beat the Christmas rush. Happy Holiday!

This type of "All Employees" message is usually posted.

There is an opening for a file clerk in the Personnel Office. Anyone interested may apply. Please contact Ann Hedrick, Extension 542.

Manager of a college bookstore posts a message to customers. The explanation of the move is intended to get sympathy and acceptance instead of a predictable resentment. There's much to be said in favor of directness, and this message suggests why.

Beginning with the winter trimester (Jan. 1974), we will charge "List" price for everything in the bookstore.

This is an attempt to offset the $70,000 loss of last fiscal year. This figure is believed to be mainly attributable to rip-offs.

If our philosophy has caused this situation, then we must all be responsible for its burden.

At the end of another year, if we find we have considerably reduced this deficit and have become self-supporting, then perhaps we can make a small discount and continue to seek the level at which we can maintain the bookstore as a *service* and not a *business.*

Until then, we all have the same bear to cross.

From a managing editor to his staff, about work schedules. Humor in dead-serious matters can replace gloomy acquiescence by smiling acceptance.

The rush hour is upon us. Despite such things as energy shortages and wars, etc., we still have a New Year's issue to put out. Accordingly, stories will be due for the New Year's issue by Friday the 14th. Monday the 17th will be the story meeting, (2:30), and stories go to production on Thursday the 20th. For those too high on holiday spirits to remember these schedules, please hand in work earlier!

About the New Year: Don't panic! There was a time when people said, "Yes, things could get worse." That day is fast approaching.

A bereavement—mother of an employee.

We deeply regret to announce the death of Carrie Nevins' mother, Grace Nevins, on Saturday, February 23.

Funeral Parlor—George Weber Funeral Home
Glendale, Long Island

Funeral Mass will be Wednesday, February 27, 10:15 A.M. at:

Sacred Heart Church
Glendale, Long Island.

From a sales promotion manager to sales representatives, announcing the details of a sales promotion plan.

Here's your chance to sell "Sweet Sixteen" like Christmas!

To really give you all the ammunition possible to make this year the biggest year for all of us, we've decided to give you and your stores complete carte blanche on the special 75% bonus offer for "Sweet Sixteen" advertising. Instead of all the requirements listed in our memo of August 6th, the only obligations your stores must fulfill are that they run a black and white ad on "Sweet Sixteen" in the time period between October 10 and December 31, and that they feature only those styles illustrated in the enclosed layout.

And please remember to send in your report

forms every week so that we can help your stores get set up for their ads.

Florence Scharf
Marketing Executive

A company president announces the availability of a new auto insurance plan. Note the specificity and clarity of details, despite the lengthy and somewhat complex message.

We have arranged with Travelers Indemnity Company of America to sponsor a "Mass-marketing Plan of Personal Automobile Insurance" for our staff members. The benefits of participating in this plan are:

1. Car insurance will be available to you at reduced rates.

2. You may use the convenience of payroll deduction to spread your payments over the year.

Your participation in this Masterplan Insurance Program will be voluntary. Your desire to do so will depend in good part on the difference between the rate you now pay and the rate that would be available to you under the plan.

In several weeks you will receive a description of coverage available and a form for requesting a quotation of cost from Travelers. If you mail the form, Travelers will advise you of the monthly cost. You can then decide if you wish to join the plan, and when. If you prefer to delay until your present policy expires, Travelers will remind you of your option thirty days before the expiration date.

To gain this service you must send in the completed quotation-request form promptly.

The plan includes a single limit of Bodily Injury and Property Damage Liability with optional limits up to $300,000, and Medical Payments up to $5,000. It also includes Uninsured Motorists protection per state law. Comprehensive damage to your car as well as Collision ($50 or $100 deductible) is optional. Towing costs up to $25 are included with each of these options. No-Fault Insurance is provided in all states where required.

We hope that you will find this Plan convenient and economical. The Plan will become operational as of January 1.

This message from an editor in chief of a trade journal to the staff combines an announcement of a meeting with an agenda item. As you know, meeting announcements often use just the first sentence of the example here. Many people are allergic to this type of cryptic communication, even find it ominous. The leavening effect of additional related business or comment warms up an otherwise cold note.

There will be an assignment meeting in the conference room at 10:30 A.M. Friday, January 11. Your critiques are due Thursday, January 10, for advance circulation. The rundown of subscriber suggestions should be helpful to us all. However, there is the danger of too many editors being inspired by the same topic. As you recall, we had several stories that overlapped last time. To avoid this, what do you think about checking in with me before you start writing so that I can keep a list of everyone's work-in-progress? Let's discuss this in the meeting.

To a large-company training staff from a program chairman about a film screening. Descriptive detail helps the recipients decide whether or not to attend.

No cheap thrills, but this Friday at 2:00 P.M. in the conference room, there will be a showing of a film on—*women! Assertive Training for Women* is defined by its producer as "an honest, direct and appropriate expression of one's feelings and beliefs in which one stands up for legitimate interpersonal rights in such a way that the rights of another are not violated." (Whew!) Illustrating this theme, the film presents eleven vignettes ranging from someone cutting into line to dealing with an unreasonably angry friend. (Get out your Psych books, Gang).

Come see the film . . . there's some interesting material here.

APOLOGY

(*see also* "I Was Wrong" *and* "You Were Right")

Something has happened to make someone angry, upset, or disappointed. Perhaps he has complained or is merely nursing injured feelings. And you may or may not be the cause or target of his resentment. (Sometimes one apologizes for a subordinate's acts.) At any rate, the aim of the message is to make someone feel better. The apt apology can turn towering rage into good feeling, convert an upset individual into one who feels better about things.

This type of message, when directed to a superior, usually has the purpose of justifying or explaining, as well as leaving no doubt about one's considered state of mind, with the hope of making it acceptable.

Warehousing manager of a plastics company writes to the head of a fabricating division explaining a service failure and suggesting that, actually, heroic efforts had been made to right matters.

I've just received your memo about the consequences of the delay in delivering a batch of .125 plastic sheets from the warehouse. Needless to say, I regret the inconvenience. Nobody likes to have people standing around. But as I mentioned over the phone, the breakdown of the delivery truck was an accident—the front axle broke when the front wheel hit a pothole. Every effort was made to cut down on the time lost. I had another truck over there pronto, with two men to transfer the sheets. I hope you'll agree that holding it to a two-hour delay was really terrific service—under the circumstances.

One manager apologizes to another for overly energetic argument and suggests a way to thrash out their disagreement by means of a discussion.

Without going into the rights and wrongs of our disagreement on the layoff problem, I do want to apologize for the turn of events in the meeting today. I guess it was the strength of my feelings on the subject that caused me to start the shouting match, and I take full blame for the whole unpleasant business.

Without calling the whole group together, I hope it will be possible for us to continue our discussion of this crucial matter. This time I'd like us to develop our points of view as alternative moves rather than as matters of absolute principle.

90

A production executive to a salesman about a missed production date. This is a model of constructive apologizing—no squirming, direct, and makes a convincing promise for future improvement.

I realize our missing the delivery date on the Morton order has put us in the hole with a very good customer. I'd like to give myself an easy way out and say that our best wasn't good enough, but that wouldn't be true. The reason for the missed deadline was my over-optimistic estimate on how quickly Fabricating could turn out that assembly. You can be sure I'll keep this failure in mind in future dealings. Meanwhile, you can assure Mr. Mackle at Morton that we'll go all out for him in the future.

A division manager assumes responsibility for the misbehavior of some of his employees and tries, with some success, to put the best possible light on the matter.

I realize that no matter what I say I can't undo the unpleasantness at the Christmas party last week. You were correctly told that the small group of young men causing the disturbance during your speech were from my department. All I can say is, they'd been celebrating a little too hard and were across the ballroom from where I was sitting. I've given each of the people involved a severe reprimand and I hope you'll agree that nothing more drastic is called for. It was clear that the audience was with you every step of the way, with the result that the noise-makers were quickly quieted.

I've talked to a number of people about the incident and I'm happy to be able to report that the interruption was hardly noticed by many. I thought your talk was very much to the point and generally well received, and the party over-all was undoubtedly a great success. I hope the New Year will bring many good things for all of us.

An executive who has let the cat out of the bag about a colleague's leaving the firm tries to right matters.

I've learned from Mr. Hendricks how upset you are that the word of your resignation is now pretty generally known. I didn't understand that you wanted it kept in strictest confidence. I must confess that I did discuss the matter with two other people, who had even less reason than I to understand that your intentions were not to be publicized. I think I know how you must feel at this point and I must tell you how sorry I am. Unfortunately there is no remedy for what I have done. I can only hope that the consequences will be less severe than you anticipate. Meanwhile, if I can be of service to you in any way please don't hesitate to call on me.

APPEALS   (*see also* Requests)

You want something done. Or you want someone to stop doing something. Because of what's involved, and/or your relationship to the recipient, you can't demand or order. In composing such a message, you often find you have to appeal to something—a quality in the person (his understanding or generosity, for example) an ideal or a principle (for the sale of greater efficiency, the good of the company, etc.).

You may want your employees to join in the housekeeping drive or you may want to ask your boss to make an exception to a company policy. Whatever the objective, the writing must sound the right notes—candor, sincerity, caring. One of the variables in this type of memo is the *strength* of the appeal—how strong to make it, how emotional, and so on. The objective, of course, is to attain a level of appropriateness. The samples that follow illustrate some of the possibilities.

Putting this notice on the bulletin board takes some of the personal sting out of the message, since no one is singled out. The absence of a scolding tone is also desirable in this type of appeal.

May we please call everyone's attention to the need to avoid littering? Halls and service rooms have been unsightly, due to the carelessness of a few employees.

Let's all of us bear down just a little more and get a big return in terms of pleasanter surroundings.

Here are two other appeals that are easily handled via bulletin board.

It's donor time again, and as in previous years, the Red Cross will set up a station in the cafeteria. Last year we had a good turnout, but it was somewhat of a dropoff from previous years. Since the benefits are substantial for all, please give this event your full consideration.

Needed desperately—volunteers to guide visitors around the plant on Family Day. All those interested, please contact Personnel at once.

This may or may not solve the problem, but what do you have to lose?

Wanted: a practical suggestion for keeping down the noise level in the cafeteria, especially when there's a meeting going on in the conference room next door. Will some genius please come forward?

An executive asks the training manager for some material for his new secretary.

I'd like to get up a reading list for Dora Wong to use to get some background on business and management. Can you jot down some suggestions—books or periodicals?

Here is an appeal for help that includes a solution—*always a welcome combination.*

Sorry to have to ask this, Boss, but I need your help in dealing with Maintenance. As I've mentioned to you several times, I'm not getting cooperation from them in emergency situations. The latest development: the Banbury mixer has been down for two days, and I haven't been able to get Maintenance to send a crew over.

What I think would be best is not just a call from you to put the bee on Muller, but a meeting in which I'd have a chance to detail the poor service we're getting. I'd hope then that Muller would make some kind of commitment that will improve things for the future.

This answers the "What's in it for me?" question.

Help! Volunteers wanted to host and hostess at the Christmas party. We can promise some fun and tons of gratitude.

The echelon problem makes this memo from an employee to his boss somewhat touchy. The writer knows he is usurping his boss's management authority. But the positive tone makes a big difference in its acceptability.

Could I possibly persuade you to reconsider your decision on Matt Durban? I agree that his showing has been decidedly poor. On the other hand, a strong case could be made to explain a good deal of his difficulty—an unfamiliar job, not enough training, and perhaps most important, not enough encouragement. I don't want to usurp any management prerogatives, but if you'd be willing to postpone his transfer, I'll volunteer to work more closely with him, help him as much as I can. I'd be glad to spell out what I have in mind in greater detail at your convenience.

A production manager writes to the head of the supply department. Note the sense of urgency he manages to create in four short sentences!

For god's sakes, Harry, get your truckers to co-operate with us! They're bringing material into my department and dumping it all over the place. A little care would help the machine operators a great deal. If you have any doubt about what's happening, stop in any time and see for yourself.

APPOINTMENTS

See Assignment and Delegation

APPROVAL

See Praise

ASSIGNMENT and DELEGATION

A major activity of managers is giving assignments to subordinates. Many of these are so short and simple, it's unnecessary to put them in writing. But in many cases it's important to put the assignment down on paper because:
 • It then becomes "official."
 • There's a record of what has been assigned—and the completed task can be compared to original objectives.
 • Your written message acts as a detailed guide of what's to be done, a road map your subordinate can use to make sure he's staying on track.
 • In some cases, notice is served on the whole group that an employee has been given a specific responsibility—by means of "copies to."

As experienced managers know, delegation is somewhat similar to assignment, but there is a technical difference. In *delegation,* an executive asks a subordinate to take over, sometimes temporarily, a task usually the direct responsibility of the executive. For example, a manager may delegate the job of screening job applicants, although he will do the final hiring. An *assignment* is a task given by a manager to a subordinate which is entirely within the job limits of the subordinate.

In this case, the assignment formalizes a state of affairs that has existed for some time.

I have today appointed Ray Lilly as acting head of the Color Room—a position he has already been filling in fact. Any matching problems can be taken up directly with him.

Here is a delegation in which the executive touches the delegatee with his mantle, and puts other employees on notice as to what's expected of them.

Pete Sweeney has agreed to take on the job of inspecting the department for appearance, neatness, and order. As my stand-in for this important job, I hope you will give him full cooperation, to the end that the department will be a credit to all of us and physical interferences with efficiency are removed.

An executive arranges for a one-week absence by telling his staff that his assistant is in charge.

I plan to be out on the Coast for the week starting February 4 to call on some of our suppliers. Please take up any questions that may arise with Fran Glidden. She knows how to get in touch with me in emergencies. Also, she can consult with Mr. Knoll if necessary. But all matters should be taken up directly with her first.

This is a somewhat different message in that it goes up the line. It's from a group of editorial assistants in a multi-magazine publishing firm to the group of editors with whom they work. The writer is Lee Glacken, senior assistant. Notice two things: first, the specificity of the assignments—who is responsible for what; and second, the fact that it's left open-ended to iron out any questions or unclear details.

Please, please, be sure that all copy which must be typed for story meetings is submitted according to the prearranged schedule: Stories for afternoon meetings should be in by 9 A.M. Stories for morning meetings should be in by 12:00 the day before. We like to oblige, but we just cannot handle the workload when we receive stories late. It makes everyone nervous and tends to make us all a little dizzy.

To help you plan your work, and to make sure editors and assistants know our division of responsibilities, here's a rundown:

Randy Thomas

Typing, copying, distributing initial copy (if any) for management publications

Retyping final copy

Dummying and reading over pages

Checking page proofs and taking all copy to production

Distributing mail, copying and handling correspondence for front-room editors.

Grace Glick

Responsible for all the above for sales publications

Dictation from editor in chief

Making arrangements for publications copy meetings

Distributing mail, answering phones, and copying for backroom editors

Responsible for typing special reports and analyses

Connie Tamara

All publications—overload typing as needed

Readership surveys (from start to finish)

All editors—miscellaneous Xeroxing, dictation

Lee Glacken

Helping all assistants, as necessary

Ordering all supplies

Expediting and filing of free-lance requisitions

Mail and telephones and copying for editor-in-chief

Responsible for all absence, personal day, vacation, weekly expense forms, copy schedules, and check requests

That's the story, folks! And if there are any questions about any of the foregoing, don't hesitate to speak up.

The head of an engineering and design department asks his staff to send along their ideas as to their overall job assignments and possibilities for change. An invitation to subordinates to express their ideas about their responsibilities makes for good participative management.

As you know, I'll be the guest of the New York State Supreme Court for the next two weeks. When I return, it will be time to think about our plans for next year.

I would appreciate getting a memo from each of you describing your present responsibilities and how you would like to see them grow or change next year. If you are perfectly satisfied with your job as it now exists, that's fine, too.

This isn't meant to be an exercise in putting anybody on the spot, merely an effort to try as far as possible to share responsibilities to the greater satisfaction of all concerned.

I hope you will all find it helpful.

This memo boils down in simple terms a discussion that may have gone on for some time and left conclusions cloudy. But now there can be no doubt of the assignment—and the date it's to be finished.

To recap our understanding reached at this morning's get-together: You will submit a plan in broad outline for the reorganization of your department so as to include the storage of your raw materials—the operation now being handled in Building #17. The report is to be submitted on or before June 30.

This longish item shows how a memo may be used as a checklist for a detailed assignment. The head of a customer-service function tells his assistant what has to be done to arrange for a meeting of customer representatives to be held on company premises. The executive has run these meetings before, which explains the completeness of the detail, but it's all new to the assistant. This memo has been included here, despite its length, because of inherent interest, particularly for those who want to set up a similar meeting.

Preparations:

Sales Department to supply list of customers to contact.

Letter to president requesting name and address of company representatives who will attend.

Follow-up by phone call if you haven't received information 2 weeks after first letter has been sent.

Invitation to conferee (with copy to company president) enclosing agenda of the meeting.

Send copies of letter, conferee, invitation, agenda, and list of conferees to head of Sales Department.

Type final roster of participants.

To Repro. Dept.

Arrange to place president and conferee letters on the Flexiwriter, to expedite mailing. Make out duplicating requisition. Letters and envelopes should be provided. Use Service Department letterhead and copies should be made of each letter.

To Purchasing

Check with Bob Eames to see if writing pads with hard covers can be provided for each conferee. Also, check on the availability of place cards for the conferee to put on the conference table before meeting.

Purchase lapel name tags (reimbursement will be made after petty cash slip for the amount spent is signed).

To Helen Keil

Keep a file of all written correspondence, schedules, lists, etc.

Keep a record of all costs.

A few days after conference, send thank-you letters to conferees.

Send memo to appropriate members of staff with preliminary report on meeting.

Make sure editor of house organ is briefed to insure full coverage.

Prepare news release for publication list.

Requisition extra copies of published material and send two copies of each issue to each of the conferees with a covering letter.

To Personnel

Phone and reserve the conference room on date needed and arrange for cleaning the night before. See that enough chairs are provided, easel paper, chalk, crayons, etc. Also clean conference room after the meeting is over.

Cafeteria Manager

Notify manager in advance—and in writing —to make the following preparations:

Coffee available to conferees for breaks and lunch.

Provide drinking glasses, pitchers with ice water.

Ashtrays.

Provide manager with a copy of the agenda for the time of coffee breaks and arrangement of lunch tables.

For Conference Room (prepare in advance):

Drinking glasses, water pitchers, ashtrays

Place cards

Enough chairs provided

Tape recorder equipment—camera
List of conferees—agenda
Pencils, writing pads, etc.
Easel chart, crayons

To Jim Breen

Discuss photographs to be taken of the meeting. Jim Breen also to check on tape recorder providing the necessary tapes.

Conference day

Two days before the conference, arrange with caterers to provide sandwiches, coleslaw, potato salad, mustard, catsup, salt, pepper, etc. Find out the cost and get the money from the treasurer's office after providing a cash advance form. The amount should include the cost of the food plus tip, and should be given to the deliverers. Make sure you get an itemized bill before payment. Tell caterer when to make delivery. IMPORTANT: Arrange to have Danish or other pastry provided for coffee breaks to be included in the food bill.

The day before the conference, receptionist should have the visitors' roster ready for each conferee to sign. Provide a list of the conferees, and lapel name tags for each. On the day of the conference, ask the receptionist to phone, on the arrival of the conferees, so they can be picked up and escorted to the conference room.

Call the mail room the day before conference to have a few empty cartons outside the conference room for garbage disposal, to be picked up that evening by the night cleaners.

After Adjournment

Wash glasses, pitchers, and leave for cafeteria manager to put away.

Have Personnel arrange to have the conference room cleaned.

Make up Weekly Expense Report, attaching bills.

AUTHORIZATION

It is within your authority to grant permission to someone to do something: an employee may take a day off, and so on. A common addition to the straight you-are-permitted message is a modification or limitation as to what may be done. This kind of memo is often important as a record, in case a subsequent question arises as to the source of the authorization.

From a department head to the personnel department about vacation-time carryovers.

I wish to authorize the carryover of the following number of vacation days for employees. These are based on inability to take vacation days during the regular period because of work pressure:

Bill Crowley   1 day
Harvey Mann   1 day
Barbara Price   4 days

Sal Russo is on vacation now, and his records are somewhat unclear. I hope we can straighten this out next week.

Head of a customer correspondence unit in a food company sends a message to head of purchasing in an attempt to clarify a matter of authorization. This is one area where failure to follow protocol can run the train off the tracks.

Although my name wasn't on the petty cash requisition, it was I who asked Ray Cone to buy the office supplies that expenditure represents. I understand that on your instruction the treasurer's office is holding up payment. I suggest that you and I take up this matter with Mr. Sayers and see if we can't get it settled once and for all. OK?

From the head of a production division to an engineer from the research and development department, denying authorization. The regrets are sincere; the reason for refusal helps make them so.

In reply to your note of July 19, I regret very much not to be able to grant permission to use our production equipment for your test runs. From what you say, I gather the materials you want to try out are unknowns, and frankly, even the slight possibility of trouble in the test can't be risked. Our machines are fully booked, and any interruptions would be a serious threat to schedules.

I am indeed sorry not to have been able to help you in this matter.

A department head asks his boss about the behavior of a peer. This is a potentially dangerous sort of memo—unless you have a special kind of relationship with your boss.

I'm pretty damn mad, and I want you to tell me if I'm wrong. Where does Pete Herr get off, calling a meeting of department heads? As far as I know, you're the only one supposed to do that. Did you give him permission? Is he assistant division manager, and some of us haven't been notified?

Obviously, what I'm saying is that Herr has just blandly taken on this responsibility on his own, and thinks he can have the name by playing the game. I think our relationship is good enough for me to blow my stack and hope for a straight answer.

An executive who is up tight for good or poor reasons tells his subordinates that they are to limit their participation in a top-level meeting. His action raises several major questions, including a key one: Does he have the authority to take such action? His move isn't recommended, for it lays him open to the possibility of blackmail by a subordinate who might leak the message to higher-ups.

We're going into a meeting tomorrow with the top executive staff to discuss plans and intentions for the year ahead. I'm going to make a request: there's to be no grandstanding or boatrocking by anyone. I would like to be the sole voice for the group, in other than minor things. In other words, no bright suggestions, no sudden brainstorms.

If you're surprised to get this kind of a note from me, for my part, I'm surprised to be writing it. But the fact is, we're in a delicate situation, with all kinds of unresolved things hanging in the balance. And I don't want to risk having the meeting go off on a tangent or into areas that are likely to be unprofitable for us in the long run.

It goes without saying that if you have any ideas or questions you'd like to discuss before the meeting, don't hesitate to contact me. There will be a department meeting following the other one, and I'll try to clarify the situation as I see it at that time.

CALL FOR ACTION

"Let's get moving" is often a keynote that precedes achievement. Action may be called for in a number of situations: You may want to take the preventive action to avoid future complications. Or your intention may be simply to start a chain of events or to help stack the cards favorably by encouraging the efforts of one or more people. A call for action may range up and down the echelons. You may be addressing such a memo to a subordinate or even to your boss—if your relationship makes such an appeal appropriate.

The wording of the message can be particularly crucial. Phrased properly, you can galvanize others into enthusiastic action. Misworded or misdirected, the message can cause resentment or a rebuff. The models below can help you pick your way through some of the hazards.

Selznick asks an assistant to check on a legal matter. Of course, the Miss Hepburn referred to is Katharine.

To: Mr. O'Shea   September 9, 1932

I hear rumors that Miss Hepburn is under twenty-one, which we should take immediate steps to confirm, to find out whether it is necessary to get the approval of the courts. I understand she is prone to exaggerate her age and likes to be thought much older than she is.

Memo From David O. Selznick

This military-sounding message did indeed originate in a military installation that was having a supply problem. The humorous conclusion is likely to win sympathy and compliance.

A contributing factor to the frequent shortage of toilet supplies is their usage by personnel for other than intended purposes. Individuals have been using paper towels for napkins, toilet paper in lieu of handkerchiefs; and soap products, both powder and cakes, have been disappearing in suspicious quantities.

Effective immediately, will all personnel please desist from using toilet supplies for other than their normal purposes? All for one and one for all.

This message for bulletin-board posting is guaranteed not to get anything but snickers. Here's why. First, the manager-writer has clearly lost his cool—in almost ludicrous fashion. Second, his attempt to get employees to inform on each other is doomed to fail. And finally, chiding the innocent along with the guilty will certainly cause resentment among the former. Traditionally, the pilferage problem is better handled by tight controls—lock and key, signing out of tools as needed, and so on, rather than by calling on people to "be honest." It should be noted that the writer is young, and new to the ways of supervision.

Hand tools have been disappearing from the cabinet at a disheartening rate. Today a five-inch micrometer turned up missing.

I ask that any person who knows anything about these thefts pass along his information to me at once. Whatever became of simple honesty? I demand that this stealing stop.

Another memo not likely to succeed. The people in the maintenance department may or may not be "dumb bastards," but the writer doesn't help his case by name-calling rather than by a recital of facts that might get his boss to act on his behalf.

Boss, can you get those dumb bastards in Maintenance to get on the ball? I've been waiting three weeks for the new control box on the #6 Press, and no action yet.

Thirty-one days hath February? A managing editor of a business publishing organization tries to prevent a repeat of an editorial disaster, by calling for several preventive actions.

Now that I'm emerging from a state of shock on finding thirty-one days in the month of February, according to our planning calendar, we'd better make some changes in the system so that this doesn't happen again.

I was certainly surprised to learn that this piece was not seen by proofreaders at any stage. Do you agree with me that all calendars that we produce should be specially checked by Proofreading?

Wouldn't it be better if we were to see flats or something before the blueprint stage on a piece like this?

Calendars have been a bugaboo with us for years, but I think that if you add proofreading to your part of the system and I add a second proof-reading from the editorial side, we may get them all right next year.

"Lateness must stop." Businesslike, even sharp, but the message avoids threats on the one hand, scolding on the other.

Folks, we just can't continue as we have been. People have been drifting in at 9:30 and even later. At ten minutes after nine this morning there wasn't a soul around.

I think you'll agree that things in the department are going too well to want to create any unpleasantness over what is basically a minor lapse. However, if it continues, it will become serious. Unless there are specific reasons, which I expect to be told about in advance, everyone should be on the job from now on at 9 o'clock sharp.

"Back the company's hobby show." The warm, hearty tone of this message is likely to dispose people favorably towards the idea of participating. To get a flood of entries, individual oral follow-up of known hobbyists would help considerably.

Where are all those hobby-horsemen? I've just heard from Personnel that no one in our department is planning to exhibit at the company's hobby show. I know for a fact, seen of my own eyes, how much talent we've got in the department. I've seen beautiful knitted wear, handsomely tailored dresses. People have brought in everything from rare coins to handmade jewelry. We all want to make the hobby show a success. And I'm sure we'd all be pleased if our department walked off with some of the prizes. Look around those home workshops, fellas. Gals, don't be shy—show off some of those handsome things you've been making. Karen Simansky is in charge of the hobby show. Why don't you contact her and tell her what you want to enter? Remember, it can be one piece or a whole collection. Get aboard and join the fun!

"Please help fill our suggestion box."

It's now a month since the company started its suggestion system. The suggestion box on my desk is nice, new, shiny, and, so far, has only a trickle of contributions. Now I know this isn't because there's a lack of ideas around. I myself have discussed half a dozen with people over the last couple of weeks. Please don't be reluctant to take that one additional step of putting your ideas down on paper. If you don't want to use the forms that are alongside the box, put your contribution down on any piece of paper. Just sign your name so we can be sure that the awards get to the right people. Listen, that's Opportunity knocking!

CLARIFICATION

This type of memo includes two forms: (1) seeking clarification of, and (2) clarifying a fact, situation, event. To satisfy their purpose, both types must be crystal clear. A memo asking for elucidation must be specific as to what's wanted; one seeking to explain must be so phrased as to be readily understood. A message intended to end confusion that itself is confused only thickens the fog.

To be realistic, however, one must recognize situations in which *lack* of clarity is intended. In such cases one depends on vagueness, digression, equivocation, and ambiguity to get one's nonmessage across. Management sometimes feels itself forced to obfuscate in circumstances where frankness might be harmful, either to the company, employees, or both. The first sample memo in this section illustrates such a situation.

Two weeks after this memo was sent out, the company announced plans to relocate to a suburban area. While technically no untrue statement was made—no final decision had been reached at the time of writing—it had already been agreed at top levels that a move would be made if a suburban property on which the planners had their eye could be obtained at a good price. Yet, the top executive who wrote this message could make a strong case justifying what was said in terms of minimizing employee upset.

A number of department managers have come to me seeking information about the progress of plans to change the location of company headquarters.

Discussion and evaluation of several alternative approaches have been going on among those who have the responsibility for this decision. One point can be made unequivocally: up to this moment, no final decision has been made.

Of course, we understand your interest and concern, and we will inform you at the earliest possible time of any news of significance. Meanwhile it should be made clear—especially to your subordinates who also may be concerned—that the decision to remain in our present location is as likely an outcome as any other.

Straight clarification. A warehouse manager to heads of fabricating departments in a plastics plant.

There seems to be some confusion on requisitioning of .125 clear acetate sheets. At present we carry two grades:

Grade A—High polish, preinspected, scratch free. Used for optical applications.

Grade B—Exactly the same material, but with slight scratches. Used for structural purposes.

If there's doubt about any application, please check specs with Engineering.

An executive is asked to clear up an assignment question.

You ask, "Which of us, George or me, is in charge of the project?" I thought I had cleared up that point. Apparently I haven't, so let me state now that *neither* of you are in charge. This decision is not a comment on your leadership ability, or George's, for that matter. My intention, frankly, is not only to get our work objectives achieved, but to see just how well two of my best people can work together shoulder to shoulder instead of as one Indian, one chief. I hope that now both my purpose and your working situation are straightened out. You can be sure I'll be readily available should any other questions arise.

Red faces in the typing pool.

Due to a typing error, a recent notice sent out by this office referring to the Scrap House omitted the first letter. To avoid mixups in the future, the structure in which waste and other materials are stored will be known as Building D.

Another clarification of a messed-up message.

Yesterday the Business Office sent out a notice reading, "Outgoing personal calls will be permitted on company lines." The word *not* was inadvertently dropped after the word *will.* Please comply with the new directive.

This executive thinks his subordinate—a new supervisor—is really doing just a so-so job. But he hopes for improvement, so fudges his "clarification."

You say you're still not clear on my evaluation of your job performance. I can't fault you on wanting to know where you stand, so here goes.

In general, you have good reason to be satisfied with your showing. The job of supervision is tough, demanding, challenging. And, as in many things, the first six months are the hardest.

I have the impression that the worst is behind you. You've had one or two setbacks—the argument with Production Control was most unfortunate—that didn't help matters. But from where I sit, as of this moment, I have the feeling that things are looking up.

I'm sure that if you continue to give the job all you've got, we'll all be pleased with the results.

An executive explains his reason for copying-in his (and the recipient's) boss.

I really don't see why you're so upset that a copy of my memo to you was sent to Mr. Gray. I always send copies of memos to him when there's a possibility of his authority being called into play. Since it's likely that our disagreement will eventually have to be laid in his lap, I thought it only proper to let him know what was going on. Of course, you have the same option.

A manager fields a colleague's question by some genteel doubletalk. Quite simply, he's in favor of the reorganization move but doesn't want to say so at this time. Three keys to the calculated vagueness are the words "possible," "unclear," and the phrase "further thought."

You've asked me where I stand on the reorganization question. Well, I'm very well aware of the operating problems we're running into, as well as the inflated costs, because of the overlap between our two departments. Do I think combining them is the answer? It's certainly a possible solution. But whether it's the most desirable one is still unclear. I intend to give it further thought before taking a stand. There's too much involved for both of us, to be stuck with a premature decision.

A top-echelon executive of a firm mak-ing disposable food-serving items clari-fies a policy decision. The memo pro-vides an interesting behind-the-scenes view of business thinking, and shows how stating both negatives and positives helps paint a clearer explanation for a policy or action. And if the message spells out factors considered, the reader is not left wondering, "Did they give any thought to . . . ?"

You have asked why it's been decided not to start a line of cold-drink plastic cups. Since your division produces cups for this market, you are entitled to know company thinking on this mat-ter.

In addition to paper cups, there is a market for the romantic features of a translucent (see-through) cold-drink plastic cup—both for vend-ing and over-the-counter use. Our intent was not to undercut our paper position but to augment it competitively by affording our salesmen as "either/or" presentation.

This we thought could be effected with our *existing* tooling and production know-how by simply altering plastic formulation to satisfy cold-drink requirements. And there would be no engineering and/or design energies taken from important product developments now in the works.

It seemed like a "natural" at the time—but we did abandon the idea after considerable deliber-ation. When you learn why we took such nega-tive action on what could well have been lucra-tive (and relatively easy) business for the plastics division, you'll agree, I'm sure, that we are completely nonprovincial in our motives.

This program was dropped when it became apparent that a plastic lid would have to be made available for these new cups.

We do have such lids, too. But they fit our hot-drink cups and necessarily sell for $3.55/M. See the rub?

If we make that same size (cold-drink) lid available at $3.55, it might cause our paper divi-sion embarrassment when their customers com-pared these lids with your cold-drink lids about the same size but selling at considerably higher prices.

Best personal regards.

COMPLAINTS   (*see also* Protests)

A message expressing dissatisfaction with a matter for which the recipient is responsible can understandably be upsetting. Too often a complaint may be seen as an accusation or as fault-finding. The fact is there are many situations in which a complaint must be voiced in order for a situation to be rectified or a worthwhile action taken. In general it's wise to avoid negative, sticky statements that may relieve the writer's feelings but increase tension. This type of memo, badly written, can sound like a graceless grumble or an unpleasant whine. But properly aimed such a message can lead to improvement —both of a situation and of feelings.

The managing editor of a publication writes to the publisher. The "you and no one else" refers to the fact that a copy of the memo is not *being sent to purchasing, since the writer hopes the publisher will take up the matter with that department.*

I am sending this memo to you and no one else. The reason is that I feel that I must be getting a reputation as a chronic complainer, and I don't relish that.

Nevertheless, the attached, using the new paper stock, represents (to me) an appalling drop-off in quality. Please note the center-spread show-through and faulty trimming. Isn't this 23-lb. stock perhaps a false economy? At the meeting where we agreed to use it, we were assured that show-through would not be any more than with the old 50-lb. stock.

If you want to do anything about it, please let me know. Otherwise I'll stick to concentrating on content.

Here's a tactful way of saying "I've been patient long enough!"

Six weeks have now passed since I first requested a report on your recent downtime experience with the new extruding machine. I know you're a busy man, I realize that this is a nuisance matter for you, but you must realize the importance of getting those figures. What gives?

From one executive to another about a touchy situation. The complaint is stated in a somewhat edgy manner, reflecting the writer's mood appropriately enough. Since the matter clearly has deep and complicated roots, the concluding sentence which says in effect, "Let's discuss," is a wise move. But note that its wording is such that the recipient is still left on the hook, and the burden of action is also on him.

I've been hoping that your arrangement to have Fay Haskins do personal typing for you after hours was temporary. But apparently it's not. Now I'm fully aware of the fact that Fay's time after 5 o'clock is entirely her own. Nor do I want to put myself in the absurd position of labeling her as "my secretary!" But I still have a feeling that the work she does for you impinges on her work and position with the company. At the very least, I think you might have raised the question with me before you created this situation. Can you suggest how my objection can be minimized?

An employee writes to the personnel officer in charge of company parking arrangements.

It takes me exactly twelve minutes to drive from my house to the plant. It takes me almost the same amount of time to get from my parking space to my office. I clocked it this morning. This is bad enough in pleasant weather, but as you will remember, we had a downpour today, and in the fifth of a mile or so distance I must walk to get from the back parking lot to my building, I arrived at my office as wet as a herring. All this is made doubly irritating because there seems to be plenty of parking space just fifty feet away from my building entrance. Would you please look into your heart and parking policy and see what can be done to improve matters?

A member of an executive staff makes his views on meetings known to his boss. Feedback of this kind to a superior requires some courage, but the risk is often worth taking, because if the complaint is justified, the writer may well come off a hero.

A lot of people think meetings are a waste of time. I'm not one of them. I've always felt meetings were a very important part of helping a company operate. But twice this week I've been stuck in a conference room as a participant —eventually unwilling—in a meeting that:

• seemed to have no purpose. After the meeting someone asked, "What was that all about?" and, you know, I couldn't tell him.

• was so badly run that on the one hand there

were long silences, and on the other, hot personal arguments.

Meetings make it possible for a lot of people to communicate with each other at once. But the same group factor also means that the amount of time wasted is multiplied by the number of people at the table.

I think we ought to take meetings either more seriously or less seriously. That is, if we're going to have them they should be run more efficiently, or else let's cut the number 'way down.

A secretary writes to her boss. Like the previous memo, this also voices a complaint aimed at getting corrective action. One might well say, "For Pete's sake, why would a secretary have to put this message down on paper? She probably sees her boss almost every minute of the day." The answer is, some people find it difficult to complain face-to-face, fearing getting emotional, for one thing. Taking the memo route makes it possible for the writer to state in a considered way what is to be said, without hesitation or interruption.

Last Friday night was the third time during the week that I had to work overtime. While you apologized and seemed genuinely sorry for the imposition, the fact is that it *is* an imposition that's causing me personal and commuting problems. Since you yourself often work late, an extra fifteen or thirty minutes may not seem like much of a sacrifice. But if I leave a minute later than 5, I miss my train, and the later ones aren't as convenient for me.

I know that often it's a last-minute request that Mr. Roman makes of you that makes it necessary for me to find a report or type a letter. And, of course, I can't blame you because he probably doesn't suspect the consequences.

I guess all this makes me sound like a poor sport, uncooperative, and so on. But if I didn't tell you how I felt, I would deserve to just go on being irritated and inconvenienced. I'm bringing up the problem in the hope that you would want to do something about it, and will.

A service isn't all it should be.

I'm sick and tired of having to bring my own tissue into the washroom. Can't we get Maintenance to do a better job of respecting one of our last few links with civilization?

COMPLIMENTS   *See* Praise

CONDOLENCES   (*see also* Regrets)

A misfortune, failure, or bereavement may call for an expression of sympathy. What you say and how you say it is a function of your actual feelings, your relationship to the individual, and so on.

This is one area of communication where the error of omission is most undesirable. Even a brief message shows thoughtfulness. Silence is likely to be interpreted as indifference.

Although, strictly speaking, most of the messages under this heading may be considered "letters" rather than memos—and might be written on personal stationery or the sender's company letterhead—they are included here as a key area of intracompany communication.

The last example, though not at all an intracompany communication, is an historic expression that has served as a model of sympathetic understanding since the day it was written.

A manager cheers up a colleague who has suffered a serious career setback.

I understand that the decision has been made not to open a plant on the Coast. Since I've seen close up how much blood and sweat you put into that project, I can realize how disappointed you must be.

But perhaps these can be two saving thoughts:

You've shown what you've got on the ball—and believe me, it's impressive. I'm sure the people up there have taken full notice.

Some worthwhile spinoff is sure to develop in the future. This company is too hot to let a guy like you fall back into a routine assignment.

So chin up, chest out! You've lost a battle, but you'll sure as hell win the war.

Maybe hospitals aren't fun, but the writer does a good job of projecting a cheerful front.

I hear you're about to join that small and select group known as the No Gallbladder Club. As a member myself, I can tell you that you're going to a hospital that has the prettiest nurses and the best meals in the world. And your convalescence will at last give you a good excuse to do what we all yearn to do, but can't because of guilt—be lazy!

Good luck. It'll all be here when you get back!

The president of a company notes the death of the father of a member of his staff.

Mr. Halley told me this morning of the death of your father. Unfortunately, I never met him, but in talking to people who knew him well, I get the picture of a richly endowed and warm human being who leaves the world poorer with his passing. Your own sense of personal loss, will, I trust, find solace with the passage of time and the many memories you must have of a loved and loving parent.

A colleague writes to one of his group whose wife has just died after a long illness.

We all share your grief. Mae was a good friend to many of us and admired by all. Please take comfort in the thought that her pain is over, something she herself wanted. And certainly, her last months of life were brightened by the endless hours of care and attention you spent at her bedside. She couldn't have had a more loving or devoted husband.

A manager writes to the wife of a deceased colleague.

It is with a feeling of shock and deep loss that we hear of George's demise. He was a most popular and well-liked friend and colleague. In the eight years of our close association, I got to know and enjoy George's wit, his good humor, and unfailing friendliness. His accomplishments were many, and his quick creative mind was a major department asset. Things won't be the same around here without him. I can appreciate your own great sense of loss. Please know that you are not alone in your mourning.

One executive sends another a mock condolence of the retirement of the lat-

Well, Agnes Warren is retiring, and after years of easy living, you're going to have to buckle *ter's secretary. The copy to the secretary, of course, is the real reason for the message—a humorous but sincere tribute to her.*

down and go to work like the rest of us. Too bad! But then, be grateful for those lush years when Agnes did everything for you from watering your plants to helping you make your toughest decisions.

You were a darned lucky fellow, and now you'll know why we always envied your having her to work with.

P.S. I'm sending a copy of this note to Agnes, of course.

On November 21, 1864, President Abraham Lincoln wrote to Mrs. Lydia Bixby, a Boston widow, to console her for the loss of five sons who were supposed to have died in service during the Civil War.

Dear Madam: I have been shown in the files of the War Department a statement of the Adjutant-General of Massachusetts that you are the mother of five sons who have died gloriously on the field of battle. I feel how weak and fruitless must be any words of mine which should attempt to beguile you from the grief of a loss so overwhelming. But I cannot refrain from tendering to you the consolation that may be found in the thanks of the Republic they died to save. I pray that our heavenly Father may assuage the anguish of your bereavement, and leave you only the cherished memory of the loved and lost, and the solemn pride that must be yours to have laid so costly a sacrifice upon the alter of freedom.

Yours very sincerely and respectfully,
Abraham Lincoln

CONFIRMATION

This is usually a cut-and-dried but extremely important type of message. It repeats or reinforces something that has already happened or been said verbally. Confirmation may refer to a past event or to a future one. In either case there are strong benefits to be gained by putting the facts down on paper: a check on original arrangements or agreements—the details, for example—and a written record. And in some cases, it's

114

a way of serving notice to someone so as to firm up a possibly shaky agreement. This is the "formalizing" effect of the written word.

An employee writes to the personnel manager.

Confirming our conversation this morning, I am to be admitted at the Hospital for Special Surgery, 535 East 70 Street—on Thursday, January 31, undergoing surgery on Friday, February 1—for ten days, followed by a recuperative period of about eight weeks.

Upon admission to the hospital I will submit the necessary hospital forms together with my identification, thus fulfilling the requirements for benefits by Equitable Life.

I would very much appreciate it if you would arrange to have my paychecks addressed to my home.

Many thanks for your kind thoughts and consideration.

A top executive answers a query from one of his staff.

We are definitely going ahead with our plans to remodel and redecorate the recreation room. The contractor tells us that the first workmen should show up on the job on the first of next month.

Training manager to a department head.

This is to confirm our phone conversation: a representative from the training service company will arrive here at 10:00 A.M. on Friday to give a demonstration of a rapid-reading course. You are one of a group of five supervisors who will pretest the program and then discuss the decision to adopt it or turn it down. See you Friday in the conference room.

A secretary to her boss.

Arrangements are all set for you to fly to Boston on Tuesday (tickets and schedule attached) and meet with Lee Bradley. He expects that four or five hours should be all that's needed to cover all aspects of the National matter.

Reservations have been made for you at the Sheraton, and when you check in you can specify the length of your stay.

I've notified Mr. Clay of your plans, and he says he'd like to see you right after you get back.

CONGRATULATIONS   *See* Praise

COVERING MEMO

This message usually makes a single point: "This is to convey to you the volume of bound reports dated 1974. . . ." A major purpose is to create a record of the transaction. Sometimes, however, the sender may also want to comment on the material being passed along: to give the recipient a context from which to evaluate what he's getting, or to make points important in themselves, in which case the transmitted material may provide a point of departure rather than merely having value in its own right.

This covering memo includes instructions for follow-up.

Attached is your certificate under the company's Long Term Disability insurance program. If you have any questions about your coverage, please write directly to the Personnel Department.

The covering memo can also be used as a means of suggesting further action.

I know you're interested in word processing. Here's an article on the subject in a magazine for professional secretaries. I guess if you really want the whole picture, best approach is to arrange to visit a firm that has installed the system.

A request for feedback.

Nice chatting with you at lunch today.

Enclosed is the type of management development material I believe we should consider, as an addition to our problem-solving meetings. What's your reaction?

An evaluation to help the recipient avoid a misjudgment.

Here's a preliminary draft of the market analysis based on last quarter's figures. I repeat, this is a draft. I'm hoping to refine it as a result of comments and criticism from several sources —you included.

An assistant from a customer relations unit sends a summary report to marketing.

Here at last is what you've been waiting for— the latest tabulation of customer profile sheets. The figures and comments in this tally represent those profiles which have been returned to us during the period of August through December by new customers of our consumer lines.

Here a covering memo raises questions and suggests a later meeting to dig into some problem areas.

I'm returning your budget proposals for next year. In general, you've done a good job of projecting needs, but as you can see by my marginal notes, some items are not clear or fail to project the realities either of growth of an activity or funds available for marginal areas. Let's clear up the problems at a meeting next Monday at 2:00.

CRITICISM   (*see also* Disapproval)

No one likes the "putting-down" effect that sometimes results from criticism. You're treading on shaky ground with this type of message.

And yet criticism is an important part of management and supervision. Sometimes there may be no improvement in an unsatisfactory situation unless criticism is made and responded to.

To get a favorable reaction to criticism, it must be made in acceptable ways. In management theory some simple principles of criticism have been enumerated: "Criticize the act and not the person," "Criticize in private," etc.

The messages below reflect some of this management wisdom and the wording by which criticism can be made constructive.

A supervisor reports to his boss (a staff executive) on the results of a planning meeting in which he was asked to partici- pate. The suggestions with which the memo closes make the earlier adverse comment somewhat less negative.

The meeting that was supposed to plan our next management get-together was a complete disaster. In part, this was due to a weak confer- ence leader. But also, every individual in the room seemed to have a different idea of what the agenda was. To be specific: Cy Tomes thought we were supposed to come up with a complete pro- gram, meeting place, and so on. Ray Gaitlin's idea was that we were just supposed to "explore possibilities," whatever that means.

I suggest that we either go back to our previous method of arranging the conference, that is, have the division heads present a finished plan, or that we appoint another committee, under a chairman who knows how to run such things.

The director of marketing has asked one of his key salesmen to review a film- strip that has been produced as a sales aid. The salesman has responded effec- tively by voicing both positive and nega- tive reactions, but then making it clear that he will try to overcome his own ob- jections to the film in actual field tests. Open-mindedness on the part of a critic makes his views more readily accepta- ble.

You asked me to give you my reaction to the new filmstrip presentation that the Promotion Department put out for the new impact-resistant plastic for sports applications. I have just viewed the strip, and I'd have to say I have mixed feel- ings about it:

Favorable. the presentation is interesting and thoroughly professional. The football scene showing our material in the form of helmets, the camping scenes demonstrating the eating uten- sils, the workshop scenes with our molded tool handles, held my interest throughout, and I don't see any purchasing people or potential users be- ing bored by what they see.

Unfavorable. I don't think this film is going to help us sell. Although there's no lack of illustra- tion of how each material is used, there's no sell, no persuasion, and also, very little information. For example, how heat resistant is our material? The camping scenes don't tell us that. What is our impact-strength? The football scenes simply show that our material can be molded into hel- mets but don't give the potential customer the facts he can apply to his own product.

One way possibly to overcome the film's faults is to have the salesman get in advance whatever application problems that prospect may have —everything from color fastness to resistance to specific chemicals, temperatures, and so on. Then immediately following the film the fact sheet can be presented.

I'm aware that after having spent a considerable amount on the film the question is not how good or bad it is but how we can use it to best advantage. I'd like to go out into the field and actually test a presentation before making additional suggestions.

After an evening out with a would-be sales representative and his wife, a subordinate writes to his boss.

Liked her, hated him. Could we give her the job?

He doesn't like a marketing survey. The simplicity and specificity of the statement makes it effective.

Sorry to be negative about the survey, but it seems minimally helpful—long on facts and figures, short on an analysis that interprets what they mean.

Although there's been a personal failure here, the writer has put the situation in an objective context, expressed satisfaction with the recipient's personal efforts, and almost created the feeling that his subordinate (a department head) has done something exemplary. You may say the circumstances justify what's said, but the fact is, the same message might have been couched in quite different and accusatory terms.

The logjam of work through your department seems to be easing a bit, and that's a tribute to your personal efforts. I know you've really dug in and done everything humanly possible to help matters. My feeling now is that if, despite all you've done, we're still in a bind, there's something about the overall workflow and scheduling that is at fault. Let's get together with Production Control and Engineering people as soon as possible to make a broader attack on the problem. I'll have Miss Blaine set up the meetings.

A supervising editor writes to a staff rookie. It's possible that the expense-account opening is just a convenient method of getting to the job review, or it may be that one thought led to the other in the writing. Either way, an apparent

If I read your expense account correctly, Anne, you have been spending practically no time and money taking prospective authors to lunch. While this may seem like a strange criticism, the fact is that there's a tradition in publishing that contracts are created over a dining table. While *remedy is in the works—which takes some of the sting out of the criticism.*

most editors in the company turn in chits for considerable weekly sums, you've been with us almost five months now and the departmental expense sheet shows no lunch charges from you.

I'm sending this along just to make sure you understand that it's expected that you take business contacts to lunch, at company expense. I don't want to put two and two together that don't fit, but perhaps a relatively low proposal rate of projects may in part relate to this lunch matter.

Now that I've said all this, I am left with the feeling that we should get together, you, Gillie, and I, to review your feelings about your job so far. What time would suit you?

A plant manager writes to one of his foremen. What makes the message palatable, in addition to the favorable elements mentioned in the beginning, is the matter-of-fact, unaccusatory tone.

I have just completed a walk-through inspection of your department, and I'd like to give you a quick rundown of my impressions.

In general, I feel you and your people are doing an adequate housekeeping job. There was a reasonably good feeling of things being in order and the work progressing without too much bottlenecking or delay as a result of poor storage or blocked aisles.

On the other hand, three conditions require prompt attention:

• Loading platform. The platform space fronting on the yard seemed cluttered with broken packing cases, temporarily stored outgoing shipments, and a discarded press that should have been sent to the scrap pile a long time ago.

• Supervisor's office. Sorry to have to mention this, Clem, since it hits close to home, but the area around your desk and the files is messy. Here I'm not talking about appearance. It's doubtful that records can be accurately kept surrounded by such disorder or that deskwork can be efficiently conducted.

• Washrooms. In a word, messy. We'll have to get after Maintenance on this.

Can we get together for a brief chat on how to eliminate these undesirable conditions?

DELEGATION

See Assignment and Delegation

DIRECTIVES

See Orders and Instructions

DISAGREEMENT

(*see also* Protests)

From time to time someone may voice an opinion, make a decision, or start an undertaking which you oppose. But the fact that you have a contrary opinion doesn't necessarily require that it be voiced or put down on paper.

As a matter of fact, disagreement may be gratuitous unless it has a purpose. (See Part I, Section 8, When Not to Write a Memo, for more on this point.) But there are times when disagreement in the form of a written statement may be undertaken:

- When your opinion has been asked for.
- When in one way or another your disagreement can be constructive.
- When for some reason you want to put your views on record.

It is sometimes difficult to keep emotions in check on an issue about which you feel strongly. Nevertheless there are usually good reasons for not giving vent to negative emotions. For one thing, such statements turn even more sour with time. In traditional management lore, it is suggested that one can "disagree without being disagreeable." Perhaps this simple rule is the height of wisdom in messages of this kind.

Plans are being made for an off-premises staff meeting and a dissenter speaks up—putting his disagreement with a majority view on a well-reasoned basis.

For the record, possibly expressing a minority opinion but one I feel strongly: I am *not* in favor of a staff meeting that takes place in a distant location. A three-hour ride with door-to-door transportation is preferable to the inconveniences required by air travel. For the period of time available, the disruption of a trip to a place like Jamaica, for example, would be a nuisance which the event does not justify.

I thought you might like to know what the grass roots are thinking.

An argument between two executives erupts in writing, and provides a good example of a poor way to disagree. This unrelieved and hostile message has all the aspects of knocking a chip off the shoulder. Instead of saying, "Let's join forces to solve a problem," it says, "Let's fight." Ironically, the view expressed is perfectly valid.

I couldn't disagree with you more. To be perfectly blunt about it, the idea that we're going to solve our absentee problem by taking it out of the hands of our supervisors and handing it over to Personnel is just plain silly.

True, Personnel must back up supervision. Working together should represent our strongest approach. But the basic responsibility must stay with our frontline managers, because they're where the action is—the problem *and* the solution.

There is usually progress made toward better understanding if the area of disagreement is clearly defined. As in this case, if the area of agreement is substantial, the differences become easier to adjust.

Apparently you've been told—by no friend of mine—that I differ with you in your view that the purchasing function should be centralized; that I favor staying with our present system.

The fact is, I do see the need for centralizing all large and company-wide purchases—items used across the board, from paperclips to typewriters.

But to cut down on delay and red tape, I believe departments should still be permitted to make small purchases, and to buy specialty items for which, over the years, they have developed their own dependable sources.

The head of an engineering department writes to the head of personnel. When there is a disagreement about something as specific as a procedure, the dissenter's best move is to offer an alternative that can be said to have some

For some time I've felt that the present method of screening job applicants is not working well for me—I'm not speaking for any of the other departments. And I know the problem arises despite your good intentions: you're trying to remove much of the burden of screening and preliminary interviewing off our shoulders. But

122

advantages over the one with which he's in disagreement.

when, as a result all I see are two or three finalists, I feel these, no matter how well qualified, represent your interviewers' idea of what's wanted rather than mine.

I'm speaking up now because I believe I have a simple change in procedure that will satisfy both of us. Next time we're hiring for my department, let me write the ad. You place it in the media you think best. Let me make the preliminary screening of responses, and you follow up on my selections. If you don't think it presumptuous, I'd like to talk to your interviewers, to stress key qualifications as I see them. They change from time to time, as you know.

Then, let me have your interviewers' results, just a brief evaluation of the survivors of the first round—and I'll make a selection of finalists and consult with you before actually hiring. How does this sound to you?

I'm sending a copy of this memo to Mr. Carlin, since he has expressed an interest in this situation.

. . . Mr. Carlin, vice-president, production, is copied-in since he may be called on to adjudicate the disagreement.

Written by a senior executive to a young Turk who, he feels, would benefit from some restraint and redirection. Despite the Polonius-like tone, the mature balance and goodwill of the message make it effective. And note the mitigating touches:
. . . the reference to their friendship in paragraph 2;
. . . the compliments, convincingly sincere, in paragraph 4, which make it clear that no adversary tone is intended.

YOU'RE WRONG ON THIS ONE, Bob—and isn't that a helluva way to start a dialog?

Of course, I'm counting on our friendship, our mutual respect, and your magnanimity to offset quickly such an abrupt—but forthright—approach to a disagreement.

Since you chose to express yourself in writing, I'll try to reply in kind; however, let's get together for a give-and-take discussion in this matter.

You do have a most refreshing spirit which this company can use well . . . and your sparkling vitality, your action-oriented drive, your rare ability—all properly channeled—will make a tremendous and healthy contribution to the continued growth of our company.

But leadership is a difficult thing to define. There are probably as many modes of leadership as there are life-styles. Good leadership has brought our company to the current level of development. Without it we could not have attained what we have at such a rapid and solid pace.

You have the fundamental stuff and the overwhelming desire—but not yet, the necessary humility . . . the leadership attitude . . . the knowledge of doing through others. You must make others feel important. You must give others their own identity, build up those around you who try. And you must temper your eagerness to make a quick track record, share the limelight which you personally enjoy so much.

It is not my intention to "take a lot of what (you are) doing away from (your) office. . . ." On the contrary, I would like to see your office grow in scope and in importance within our company. And this can only be done if you begin to realize fully how very important it is for you to learn from those around you and cause them to want to see your position expand. True, authority can only come to you through the efforts and desires of others; it cannot be done by edict or by force. In the long run, earned respect alone is the omnipotent force which makes the leader.

. . . note how the "you and I" paragraph takes some of the sting out of the message, making it easier to accept.

You and I both are afflicted with the same frustrating malady of impatience with people. We must control our active desire to run singly. We must consult and we must subordinate.

So, Bob, do your thing—the right thing in this important matter—insist that each man do his job . . . help him do that job . . . let him take credit and recognition for doing.

The building of people is our most important task at this time. Doing it properly—I am convinced—will give us the biggest and the best return in both personal satisfaction and company growth. THAT'S LEADERSHIP!

DISAPPROVAL   (*see also* Criticism)

There's a lot to approve of in organizational life, and there are also reasons for disapproval. Approval is like Sunday afternoon in the park with the kids: nothing bad is likely to happen. But a memo of disapproval is a message bound to meet with a certain amount of touchiness at the other end. In some cases, reactions can be explosive: a boss hits the ceiling and wants to know what the writer thinks he's doing; a subordinate quits, etc.

But disapproval, as a form of criticism, can also be constructive, helpful. The samples illustrate some of the notes that can be struck.

A production manager writes to a sales executive explaining the problems he's having with a form report originating in the sales department. The memo pulls no punches, and shows the difficulty of making "something's wrong" sound like a good-news message. But the key point is that what's said is important feedback, and can lead to helpful action.

I am returning this "Contact Report" to you and hope we can discuss it together. The reason is that the whole business of customer contacts is very badly organized—at least from where I sit.

Obviously, somebody should be contacting General Foods. I am also attaching a copy of a letter from Allied Chemical. As you can see, the notes in red ink don't tell me anything, and I have no idea who sent it to me, or who Sandy is, or whether she wrote them or sent them the copies they asked for.

It seems to me vital that we should have a meeting with the people who receive these letters and set up some more organized method of handling them, passing them on, etc.

Let us do this soon. As you well know, poor handling of correspondence can build mountains of ill will.

An executive feels he's not getting anywhere in a hiring move. At least, a suggestion is made that can improve results.

I'm less than pleased with the quality of the job applicants I've been seeing. As I thought I explained, the position now open on my staff has a big future and must be matched by a new employee with a big potential for growth.

Can we start over, run a new ad—with my office given the opportunity to review the wording?

A sales manager draws the line at what he considers high-handed decision-making by a purchasing agent. There is a strong tone of fault-finding that obviously goes beyond the matter of the attaché cases, to other past disappointments.

I must insist that you return the fifty attaché cases you recently bought for our salesmen. I don't think these are the kind of cases that will add prestige to our men in the field. I understand that you made the decision on your own because I was out on the Coast when the purchase was made, and I do realize the price factor is an important one. Nevertheless, my assistant, Jim Curran, was available for a final OK of the sample. He had the authority to make the final decision but he was not consulted.

. . . and then we learn that the writer is basically concerned with the question of authority and responsibility.

Of course, my point, above and beyond the matter of this one purchase order, is that a decision was made without consulting the people who should have the final say. It is my department's responsibility to prepare and equip the men in the field, not anybody else's. You may remember that a similar situation arose in connection with the binders for our sales brochures. At that time I reluctantly went along with a poor choice—one that was made without anyone in my department seeing final samples.

. . . since one can't expect all working relationships to be suffused with sweetness and light, perhaps the writer deserves some points for putting the situation on a realistic basis.

Another way of looking at this, Greg, is simply to say that the money for these purchases is coming out of my budget and I expect to have the final word. I hope this explains both my feelings in the matter and what I look for in our working relationship in the future.

From head of merchandising to an art director. Question: Can a message disapproving something for which the recipient is responsible be sweetened up without phoniness? One way: be firm about the fault, but minimize the consequences, as, "another try should get us what we want without too much trouble." And avoid gratuitous overstatement: for

I'm somewhat disappointed with the formats I saw yesterday. They were, in my opinion, below our standard. Please do not infer criticism of the artist from those comments—after all, he has only been here a few days. However, I think it might have been helpful if I had known he was starting the project and could have given some guidance. However, another try should get us what we want without too much trouble.

example, the word "far" was edited out before the phrase, "below our standard."

In general, it is best simply to voice dissatisfaction matter-of-factly, and suggest a meeting to iron out difficulties. That is, unless the intention is to spell out for the record a problem at length.

I am attaching some of our past formats, which he may or may not have seen. These are only for "feel" and of course not to be copied.

The quality that has always worked best for us is dignity and elegance. The jazziness of the submissions, the use of dollar signs, for example, seems out of keeping with our image. Can we get together to discuss this—possibly with your new artist included?

DISMISSAL   (*see also* Resignations)

"In each life the ax must fall," says one punning executive. From time to time a manager may have to fire a subordinate and in some cases the announcement of the firing has to be put in written form.

But there is a vital legal aspect to this kind of message that must not be ignored if the writer and his company are to avoid the possibility of a suit for libel. Here's what's involved:

Technically you can tell a firee anything—"You're being fired because you falsified records . . .," for example—that explains your action. But it's crucial that no one else overhear—or read—your statement. In one case where an employee was notified by mail that he was being fired because of lying and dishonesty, his wife read the message, and so provided the basis for a suit.

Practically, then, it's unwise to make any *defamatory* statement in connection with dismissal: "You're a liar" . . . "a crook," and so on. The truth of such statements is a defense, but it may have to be proved in court.

Even though "qualified privilege" permits you to explain dismissal for a possibly libelous reason to a select few—the head of the personnel department, your boss, a key union representative—it still is unwise to commit this message to writing—which, even if marked confidential, might fall into improper hands. It is this legal consideration that warrants use of euphemistic language: "Your services will no longer be required . . .," etc., even to people you're letting go for serious breaches of conduct.

In other situations, dismissal may involve strong feelings. The executive doing the firing and writing the memo may feel anything from glee to profound regret. And the attitude of the recipient also may cover a range of feelings from indifference to deep shock. A further complication: There might have been a close working relationship, indeed, a friendship, between the firer and the firee. Obviously such a relationship must figure in the tone of the message.

The samples in this section cover some of the possibilities and suggest wording that can suit this difficult area.

A department head of a toy company announces termination of an employee. The use of "resignation" to explain a ter- mination, even as here, where the em- ployee has been forced to leave by elimi- nation of her job, is generally accepted as a graceful euphemism. Of course, an employee who quits summarily may lose unemployment benefits, so the official re- cord must be clear on this point.

I regret to have to announce the resignation of Linda Derringer. Linda's resignation flows from the fact that we have decided to discontinue pro- duction of special hobby materials.

Linda has agreed to stay on for a period of four or five weeks in order to tie up loose ends, espe- cially customer servicing. We shall miss her sorely and wish her the best for the future!

A somewhat impersonal announce- ment is sent to an employee who has been with the company a short time. Note that the reason for the firing is not mentioned, and within the context of the message, is not needed. This does not preclude the employee taking up the question, if there is one, with his supervi- sor or the personnel department.

It is with regret that I must tell you that your employment with the ABC Company will termi- nate on February 22. Please contact Mr. Cham- bers in Personnel to arrange for your separation check and related matters.

An automotive parts plant announces a general furlough.

Due to a shortage of supplies, the plant will be shut down from April 5 until the supply situa- tion can be overcome. This applies to all shifts. You'll be notified of start-up at the earliest possi- ble time.

Manager of a bookstore gets a load off his chest, spells out his reasons for firing, and then lets the ax fall. He probably felt great about this memo. But the employee might cause some skipped heartbeats by

Because I have spoken to you repeatedly about your lack of responsibility to the job; because you called someone not even connected with the bookstore to ask to work your hours for you; be- cause you did not even consider that your co-

128

threatening a libel suit. Best advice when you fire an employee who, you feel, fully deserves the gate: Be matter-of-fact rather than emotional, put as little as possible in writing.

In this dismissal memo the two principals are obviously on friendly terms. Note how the writer has said what had to be said and yet put the entire message in an acceptable framework. The reminder of a continuing relationship can be most helpful.

worker maintains a part-time job because she cannot work a full-time one. Because you did all this at the most essential part of the season. Because you did not even call to tell me that you had changed your plans yet again. Because I sense that you really want to be rid of your obligation to the bookstore. Because all this epitomizes the reason why I once said you can do anything you want, but it might not be in the bookstore and you might not get paid for it—you are fired.

You are free to appeal to whatever access there is if you feel my decision is unfair.

Ken, this is one memo I never thought I'd have to write. And I want you to know that it is one of the most painful things I've ever had to do in my business career.

But I've just had a long conversation with J. P., and although he's personally well disposed to you, he says there's no alternative than to have you leave the company. This decision has been made without my participation. And yet I can't divorce myself from it. You and I have had several talks about the poor results shown by your department. Repeated initiatives and promises for improvement just haven't panned out. There's not the slightest doubt of your capabilities. Accordingly I feel that the future is likely to be considerably brighter than the past has been.

I'm trying to avoid that old phrase, "This is the best thing that can happen to you." I know that you'll be leaving many good friends and well-wishers behind. On the other hand, my own feeling now is that there has been something wrong about the chemistry of the situation.

J. P. has agreed that you be given any reasonable time to find a new affiliation or to develop your career plans. You know you can count on me for any assistance now or later on.

"DROP DEAD!"

You have been moved to annoyance, irritation, anger, by someone's unacceptable behavior. It may be obtuseness, viciousness, insensitivity. Whatever the reason, your reaction is strong enough to make you want to get rid of an emotional head of steam. Company politics being what it is, this type of memo is usually not sent to a superior—unless it's preliminary to an offer to quit. And it is usually not sent to a subordinate since it suggests an abuse of one's power and authority. This leaves only those at one's own level as possible recipients.

Before you send this type of memo, look over the samples in this section with a calculating eye. When you find one that reflects your feeling, ask yourself one question: "Do I really want to say something like that?" If the answer is yes, just hesitate a moment longer and ask, "Will I be sorry tomorrow?" If the answer is no, go ahead, but consider it a contribution to your mental health rather than a constructive company communication.

A production manager registers his annoyance with a continuing complaint from a manager of an adjoining department.

I have just gotten your third note about removing the employee coat rack from the corridor outside my department. I agree that it doesn't do great things for appearances, but I have to remind you that this is a factory and not a showroom. If you can get Walters to provide a suitable alternative I'll be glad to use it. Meanwhile, please don't mention this matter again, unless you can come up with some satisfactory way of handling it.

A young executive tells off a would-be competitor.

I'm still steaming about your behavior in the meeting this afternoon. Your interruptions to my presentation were obstructive and uncalled for. You can be damned sure that I was perfectly willing to field any questions or objections after I'd finished. But to have you continually jumping up and making comments made it impossible for me to finish before the meeting was over.

At our next weekly meeting Bill assures me I'll have the chance to complete the presentation. He also apologized to me for not controlling the meeting better. He's agreed to make it clear that

I'm to proceed uninterrupted until I finish what I have to say. But I think you've done the whole group a disservice by your tactics and I want you to know just how I feel.

Sarcasm is a deadly weapon—but it can be double-edged. Think twice before putting this sort of message on paper.

Nice work, Ken. With a customer standing by, you go out of your way to put me down and make the bank seem to be run by nincompoops. Next time you have the impulse to put on a display of poor judgment and bad taste, let me know and I'll arrange to have a bigger audience present.

This is a curious message. If the recipient has an inclination to fix the sender's wagon by showing it to higher-up Crandall, he may be raising questions about his own behavior. The threat at the end is out of a Gothic novel and is meant to make the bad guy of the piece turn a hair or two.

You'll be delighted to know that a new office manager has just been hired from the outside. When Crandall announced the news, he at least had the decency to tell me he was sorry and say that nevertheless I still had a good future with the company.

It's been no secret between us that you did what you could to swing Crandall around to his decision. We both know I could have handled the job, and I deserved it. Purely personal feelings influenced your attitude. Well, you've won out. I hope any satisfaction you have over the outcome will be short-lived.

ENCOURAGEMENT

Telling a person that he's doing well or making clear your faith in his capabilities can be a most heartening message. Many a successful individual can point to the kind words of a colleague or boss at a critical time that proved most helpful. The person who faces a tremendous challenge or one who is floundering, or indeed one who has failed in some way, can find in a properly worded message understanding and reassurance, a new strength, and enhancement of his capabilities.

In some cases, the message may be sent to a family member, and typically, concerns the health or prospects of the employee.

And some messages that are basically informational may be treated in such a way as to become spirit-boosters, and as such, highly motivating.

A vice-president lays it on the line for a young protegé.

I'm not going to give you any of that darkest-before-dawn malarkey. The fact is that you tied your future to a star that didn't get off the ground. The company has taken a $200,000 bath, and your faith in a new product proved to be misplaced.

Now you can do one of three things:

Start looking for another job.

Stay on and hope to slowly build yourself back to where you were in status. That should take about three or four years.

Stay on and act as though you've come out on top of a tough struggle. Demand a new and challenging assignment, based on what you've learned.

My advice is to take course No. 1 or No. 3. I'm strong for No. 3 because as I see it, you tackled an impossible job and came pretty damn close to pulling it off. In the process you acquired experience this company can benefit from.

I'm counting on you being a V.P. in this outfit one day, and I told Mr. Miller so. Don't make a liar of me, Walter, when you see Mr. Miller to discuss your next step.

A vice-president sends a note to the wife of an employee. The personal nature of the message takes it outside usual intraorganization limits, but it's the kind of expression one is sometimes called on to make because of one's position. Personal stationery of some kind should be used for condolences and other personal statements.

I know only too well—from my own recent experience—the very troubling situation in which Frank's heart attacks have placed him, you, and your entire family.

It's most difficult at a time like this for anyone to do more than try to help you through these days by reminding you of the warm feeling that so many of us have for all of you.

What furthermore can we do except say, "Tomorrow will be better"?

A little over a year ago I experienced what Frank is now going through. Thankfully, for many months now I have been back on a full work schedule—with a new found realization of how important life itself is . . . how important my work is to me . . . and, perhaps, how more important than everything are those commonly referred to as "loved ones"—and how much they really mean to me.

So, Mrs. Pearson, in one sense I can make the meaningful statement that I'm a lucky man; for God has been good to me.

We're all praying for you and Frank and your family. Please, extend our personal and corporate best wishes to Frank for a good recovery from his recent ordeal.

Best personal regards.

Success is always encouraging.

The third quarter's figures are in, they're better than last year's, and in my opinion, we're going up! Keep plugging and I believe we'll all be delighted with the results at year's end.

A boost for a departing colleague.

Just got the announcement that you're leaving us. Behind the bland words I gather there's a lot of blood, sweat, and tears. My impression is that the job just wasn't right for you.

That you're a person of many strong talents I had the occasion to learn during the times we worked together on a few projects. So here's hoping your next job is a better fit and will permit you to give it what you've got. Best of luck, and don't hesitate to call on me if I can be of help. Keep in touch.

An alcoholic is coming back to work after five months of drying out and therapy. The message is from his immediate superior.

Mr. Foster tells me that you'll be coming back to work next week. Just to let you know that all your friends and colleagues will be happy to see you, and we're eager to have you do your old job with the special distinction you always brought to it. And personally I'm very pleased that we'll be working together again.

EXPLANATIONS

See Clarification

FAREWELL

Someone is leaving. It may be temporary or permanent. It may be a result of a resignation, retirement, or transfer. It may be a subordinate, your boss, or you yourself. At any rate, a departure uncelebrated or unnoticed is not likely to do justice to one's emotions or a relationship. What is said, of course, will reflect the nature of one's feelings and the quality of the relations between the sender and recipient of the memo. The examples that follow put the writer in both roles—as the departing individual, and as the writer of the message to one who is on his way.

A colleague's resignation from the company calls for a friendly send-off. Note in this letter the simple directness of what is said and coincidentally the absence of stilted words or sentiments.

I just read Mr. Bradley's announcement of your resignation. My sense of loss is immediate, strong—and selfish. I know the announcement says that you are going on to bigger and better things with another organization. I hope this is literally so—in which case I wish you the best of luck, and I do hope that you leave with only minor regrets.

For my part I shall certainly miss you. Although we never had the occasion to work closely together, it seems amazing to me now that in the ten years of our acquaintance our contacts were either in the cafeteria at company functions or in the men's room.

But feelings do not need too much to grow on. I always felt we were good friends. Your reputation in the company is outstanding, and I'm sure the respect and regard in which you are held have been fully deserved.

So, again, all the best for the challenges ahead, and add my name to the long list of those who were glad to have you as a colleague.

Here's a sincere and friendly good-bye to a colleague who is retiring. The giving of a special gift, of course, emphasizes the personal feelings of the sender. This message neatly avoids the maudlin and

We didn't have much chance to talk at your great send-off party last night. But I did want you to know what a great affair it was. I hope your retirement will be the beginning of all kinds of worthwhile activities.

134

emphasizes the positive aspects of retirement. The "I'll miss you" note is absent here, but where it is appropriate, it should be included and stressed to the extent desirable.

As you promised in your speech, I expect you will be coming back to visit your old friends every once in a while. You are one person I certainly don't want to lose touch with. And, just to make sure you won't forget our many years of working together, you will be receiving a small token that I hope will serve two purposes: first, remind you of our friendship and, second, bring to you some of the pleasures of nature and the outdoors. It is an unusual book, *The Spirit of Wood,* by Eric Sloane.

I trust that reading it will be one of the many pleasures that will be coming your way in the days ahead.

In this memo the sender is the person who is leaving. Too often when people go away they do so without a farewell word or gesture—which may create an unintentional vacuum. A message, even one as brief as this, prevents such an unnecessary breach in personal relationships.

As you can imagine, things are pretty hectic in getting ready for my new assignment overseas. But I wanted to put down on paper my gratitude for your interest and helpfulness over the years. You will remember you were my first boss. As a matter of fact, you hired me into the company—a move for which I've had good reason to be grateful.

I hope we can keep in touch, at least through the mails. I'll drop you a line when I get located in London. And, of course, I hope things continue to go well for you. You're a great guy and deserve all the best.

Here's a message that cannot help but please the person to whom it is sent. This memo does a good job of wishing the recipient well and adding a note of reassurance about the future.

Lou Wald tells me you are leaving for another job. Of course I'm annoyed that you didn't let me in on your big secret. You only worked for me for a few months, but you were the best secretary and assistant a manager ever had.

I'm sure you are making a right move. You had a helluva lot more on the ball than the organization has been able to recognize.

I hope your new job is a giant step upward and gives you the chance to exercise all those managerial ideas you've always shown. Good luck and congratulations to the fortunate organization that gets you.

FIRING

See Dismissal

FOLLOW-UP

Follow-up memos tend to be of two kinds:

- There has been a previous message or action to which there has been an inadequate response, or desired results are lacking.
- A previous message has been sent or an action taken, and there is more to be said on the subject.

The follow-up memo can be particularly important in keeping alive a subject or an activity that might otherwise fade away. It also serves to provide feedback on past actions.

Brevity does the job when the recipient knows what's at issue.

Still waiting . . .

Follow-up of an office redecorating project. An office manager reports to his superior.

Here's to bring you up-to-date on the physical changeovers of the office:

- I've made several floor layouts, trying to work out the best locations for the five desks and the files.
- Purchasing has had two office-furniture salesmen up here, and I've gotten their suggestions for types of desks and files. One had an interesting idea for a large circular file, which might work out for us.
- Mr. Scheff, a decorator who is recommended by Purchasing—I think he did your office—is due in next week to discuss drapes, carpeting, lighting, and colors for walls.

After the preliminaries, I'll show you two alternative plans—least expensive, most expensive—and I expect we'll be able to decide on a final version. I'm hoping to have the proposals finished by a week from next Friday.

"Help!"

We're stopped dead on the Acme order until we get the A-17 subassemblies from you. Will you please let me know at once when these can be expected?

This morning I concluded an interview with the last of the three job applicants you screened for us. You've done a good job, and all three were good possibilities. At this point, my preference is for Dan Huysman. His experience seems to be better suited to our needs, and he has a bright manner that should be an asset out in the field.

Since this is a key job we're filling, I'd like to minimize our risk as much as possible. Would you contact Huysman and see whether he'd be willing to take a battery of psychological tests? No pressure, of course, and I'd be surprised if he said no. My intention is to hire him unless there are strong negatives in the psychological.

As of this date we have completed eight out of the twelve lots we're processing for American. Last four are due for completion end of the day, March 4. You can arrange your shipping schedules accordingly.

On July 7 we had a meeting at which we agreed that you would order an A-frame for our compression press, since a slight crack had developed in machine #6. Two days later, the frame gave way, and the machine has been out of operation since.

One July 23 I called you on the phone and urged you to expedite delivery of the A-frame from the manufacturer. You said you would do so.

On August 3 I called you again, and you admitted that you had failed to follow up the original order but would do so immediately.

On August 10 I visited you in your office, and you showed me a letter from the Dumont Company saying that delivery of the frame would be made by August 20.

Today, September 3, the frame has been on the premises for almost two weeks, and you have not yet scheduled the machine repair. What I want to know is, when the f--k are we going to get that press running?

GRATITUDE

Appreciation falls as the gentle rain from heaven on the parched place beneath. Recognition is one of the holy grails of corporate life, more sought after than found. Anytime you have the chance to express thanks to someone, you can be sure, whether the message is aimed at your boss or a subordinate, it will be taken as an indication of your thoughtfulness and sound character. Twin hazards are effusiveness and a bare-bones "thank you" that may not do justice to the situation. In composing an expression of gratitude, answers to two questions can supply subject matter: *how* you feel—"In my ten years with the company, nothing else that's happened matches your consideration . . ."; *why* you're grateful—"Your thoughtfulness now makes it possible for me to . . ."

Gratitude for off-the-job consideration.

Now that I'm back at work, after three weeks of hospital incarceration, I want to tell you how grateful I am for your visits. They certainly brightened the days. And the azalea you sent is adorning my desk this very moment, a permanent reminder of your thoughtfulness. I would say the fringe benefits in this company are tremendous!

Appreciation of help in winning advancement.

We both know that promotions in this company are earned. And I'd have to agree that when the news came through today, my satisfaction included a certain amount of feeling that justice was being done. But I'd have to be both stupid and ungrateful if I failed to recognize the full extent of your contribution. Starting from that day three years ago, when you sat me down and gave me a picture of what the possibilities were for me, and the countless times since that you helped with sound advice and encouragement, your efforts on my behalf made all the difference.

I'll never forget your kindness, your friendship, and your wisdom.

Appreciation to a boss for praise in an especially important circumstance.

That was certainly a great buildup you gave me in the board meeting this morning. I want you to know that my hat still fits—for two reasons:

Only a great boss can have great subordinates.

We both know that it has been your help and encouragement that moved me along every step of the way.

As the song goes, you made me what I am today, I hope you're satisfied. I am—and very grateful as well.

Victim of a reorganization due to a business downturn—in effect he's been demoted—expresses appreciation for kind words from a colleague.

As you can imagine, these are pretty dismal days for me. At the moment, I'm not sure whether I'm going to continue to be an employee of this company—my decision. Mr. Davis has indicated that he hopes I'll stay on.

Your words of cheer and wisdom are a bright spot in an otherwise gloomy picture. Just knowing there's a guy like you around may prove a major factor in my decision. But whichever way the decision swings, thanks for your thoughtfulness.

A saleswoman tells a marketing executive how advertising efforts have paid off.

When I used to go into a new store I'd introduce myself and then I'd take a deep breath so that there would be no hesitation after I'd said that I represented Teenform. I had to hasten to explain the kind of merchandise the company offered.

Now I can take my time in going into the product. Teenform *is known*—thanks to your efforts.

The advertising that we are getting now makes it not only easier but more pleasant for us.

Source: Florence Scharf, Marketing Executive

A salesman responds to a note from his boss congratulating him on his fifth anniversary with the company.

Thanks for your note. I certainly appreciate the nice things you said—and I'm not so humble that I didn't get a big boot out of your praise. You know, this is the third firm I've sold for, and I'd be lying if I didn't come right out and say it is the best. And, of course, you're a part of that.

I believe this will be my best year. At least I'm going to put all I've got into the attempt to make it so.

This expression of gratitude avoids the usual pappy suggestion that all is peaches and cream, in favor of an honest statement of the writer's doubts. From a political standpoint, however, such questioning of corporate wisdom and the registering of any but gung-ho enthusiasm might be hazardous. The determining factor, of course, is the organizational atmosphere. If open and enlightened, the writer deserves high marks for intelligently stating his feelings. In a less open situation, the message might better have been oral, or closed with the phrase, "Please destroy after reading."

Thanks very much for your note about my new assignment. I do appreciate your kind words, particularly since I'm not sure myself whether switching from a desk job into customer field service is a promotion or a demotion! But you've persuaded me that it's probably good, in the long run, for me to be pushed into something new. Thank you for helping me see the light—I hope.

"HELP, PLEASE!"

See Appeals *and* Requests

HIRING

(*see also* Announcements)

This is a special form of the announcement memo but deserves separate treatment because of its unique message—which can be crucial. When a new employee comes aboard, particularly in the upper echelons, *how* his arrival is presented to others can make a great difference in the reception he gets. One might think that the warmer, the more glowing, an introduction, the better for the new arrival. Often the opposite is true. Too big a buildup can be a handicap. Expectations from colleagues become too high. And peers, threatened by a heralded superman, set out with axes to set matters aright. Best approach is a balance between too flat understatement and overblown fanfare. In a pinch, the former is preferable.

A company president announces the appointment of a key company executive. Doubtless there is more that could be said about Shipley's qualifications, but the writer wisely uses restraint to avoid overselling—which almost always causes resentment.

Effective immediately, Greg Shipley will assume the post of Treasurer, reporting to me.

Until this appointment, Greg served as an officer of the Walters Company in San Francisco, in the capacity of General Accounting Manager and Assistant Secretary. He is a native Californian, a Dartmouth economics major, and a C.P.A. Previous to joining Walters, he was a senior accountant with Smith & Dover.

Greg Shipley will supervise the Accounting Department, the Business Office, and our Data Processing operation.

I know we will all want to welcome Greg to his important new responsibilities.

The personnel department sends an announcement to all department heads, to be posted.

Starting Monday, June 3, there will be a new face at the reception desk. Mary Kemp recently graduated from St. Thomas High School and is known to many of us as a summer trainee. We're all delighted to welcome Mary Kemp, and we know the receptionist responsibility will be in capable hands.

From the president of a book publisher to the staff, announcing the hiring of a new editor. Providing a brief rundown of previous affiliations is more or less traditional and suggests the qualification for his new position.

I am delighted to announce that, effective Monday, January 22, Henry Lucas will join us as Sponsoring Editor. It is anticipated that he will, in general, assume all editorial responsibilities previously held by Tom Lauter.

Henry brings a wealth of experience to the job —including sales and advertising service with the University of Chicago Press, Cambridge University Press, and the Free Press of Glencoe. More importantly, he served as editor in the Reference Department of the Van Allen Press. Please join me in welcoming him into the company.

A manager alerts his staff to the arrival of a new staff member.

You'll be pleased to know that at last we've been able to fill the spot vacated by Mel Corbin. Our new colleague, Harriet Stella, is well qualified for the job, and I'm sure will prove to be a valuable addition to the staff. I'll see to it that you meet her personally soon after she joins us.

A company president announces the appointment of a director of employee relations. A bit of tub-thumping for the organization also contributes to a positive tone for this type of message.

The significant growth of our company during recent years has greatly increased the responsibilities which normally fall within the Personnel area. Personnel Director Henry Roos has for some time urged that we expand our ability to meet these growing needs.

I am pleased to announce today, Monday, December 3, that Helen Waldo has joined our staff as Director of Employee Relations. Henry Roos, as Personnel Director, will continue to carry the responsibilities he has ably performed. With the addition of Helen Waldo to the staff, we can now assure ourselves that we are doing all that we are able to toward effective relationships with and among the members of our large and growing staff.

Ms. Waldo brings to this assignment a substantial background in manpower planning, organization analysis and development, and management development. These were among the responsibilities she carried at General Paper Company. More recently at Gretchen & Company, a well-known management-consulting firm, she was in charge of their entire internal employee relations and training activities.

The addition of Helen Waldo to our management staff is certain to be especially helpful in a period of years which will be complex for us. With Henry Roos as Personnel Director and Helen Waldo reporting to me as Director of Employee Relations, we can be confident that we are equipped to do the job facing us.

To someone unfamiliar with the world of business, this may seem like a fine introduction. But the chances are that unless Mr. Emerson has the wisdom of Solomon and the dexterity of an eel, his grave has been dug. The inflated image that has been presented, the implied put-down of present staff members, who are made to seem like inept dullards who couldn't lick a postage stamp, are bound to get Ralphie the coldest shoulder on record. And this will be true even though he may be as good as advertised.

We've been extremely fortunate in acquiring the services of Ralph Emerson to take over as chief of the copywriting function. Under his able guidance we're sure to eliminate the deficiencies we've all been aware of and have been unable to overcome. Ralph Emerson has an outstanding reputation in the industry, and we're bound to benefit from his tremendous energy, creativity, and general know-how.

Ralph will be joining us the first Monday of next month. Be prepared to welcome an outstanding new colleague.

IDEAS (*see also* Persuasion; Proposals; *and* Suggestions)

Ideas, suggestions, and proposals are three related categories. An idea may be communicated for a number of reasons other than as a basis for a suggestion or proposal—for example, for the record. An individual may have an idea that he wants to get down on paper just to preserve it. He may want to send it along FYI (For Your Information), so that another individual may also be aware of it. Or, an idea may be described to another person because it is incomplete and perhaps that individual can help in its development. The models below show some of the ways in which this type of material can be handled.

A senior staff member writes to the head of the group.

I'm sending this memo along to you on the assumption that half an idea is better than none.

We both have been troubled by the low morale, even the apathy, of the staff recently. Maybe it's seasonal, maybe it's something seeping down from the higher echelons.

But I think an informal get-together after hours—for whatever plausible, constructive reason you can suggest—might provide an opportunity for people to open up and reveal reasons for the gloom.

You can be sure the addressee—in charge of a training-services organization—will bite on this one. The sender had better have the stuff.

I've got a great idea for a new cassette series addressed to a large, training-minded audience. I've been putting together some facts and figures and would like the opportunity to discuss these with you at your convenience.

An observant foreman writes to his boss.

We've all been trying to figure out how such things as five-gallon cans of paint, hand tools, and even an adding machine have been disappearing from the plant, despite what seems to be pretty good security. Well, I'm no Indian tracker, but this morning I found a Stilson wrench that had been dropped near the back fence, and there were a lot of footprints in the wet dirt. I think the stuff's been going over the wall. Can we investigate?

Ideas need not always be fully developed. Note this from a sales executive to his promotion manager, about a means of rekindling enthusiasm in a somewhat dispirited sales force.

In my judgment, the business climate that we're operating in represents about 90% of our problem. The typical business executive is just so damned upset about the energy crisis, inflation, etc., that he doesn't want to listen to any sales talk. And even if we get in, we just can't seem to focus his attention on taking any action.

Quite candidly, I don't know what to recommend, but I do know that it's our responsibility to keep the salesmen as excited as possible about the opportunities that exist in just this type of business climate. After all, our system offers low-cost security improvement at a time when

144

pilferage, etc., may reach new highs. I'm just wondering if you could come up with some sort of special brochure entitled "New Security Needs in a Period of Business Uncertainty."

Recognize that this is all very vague, but I'm looking for anything that will give us leverage and build a head of steam.

A top executive in a plastics firm sends a memo to a fellow staff member describing a new merchandising idea and asking for his reactions. Notice that the message is loaded, that is, the writer presents the idea in rosy terms. Cricket? Well, people have a way of falling in love with their own ideas—and want them backed by others more often than they want them evaluated—despite what's said.

We're kicking around a thought—and we would appreciate your personal comment and advice prior to our making any decisions in the matter.

With our plastic cutlery we're enjoying a pretty darn good sales response—even with a short line and no "push" behind it. And—in April we'll add a soup spoon, and an eight-inch soda spoon will come in May. So, very soon we'll really be in the business.

Even this early in the game we've already felt a thundering pulse of big volume. True, it's a most competitive and price-conscious business. But these items do complement our other products and do tend to make us a one-stop-service source of supply in addition to increasing our dollars of sale.

So, what if we went to market with a larger size so-called economy pack (2,000-, 2,500-count, or even more) plastic *spoons,* and our savings of packaging material and handling were passed on to the customer? It might amount to 5¢ per M. Such innovation could help give us some promotional and leadership value in the industry, too.

It would seem from our recent experience, at least, that those who use plastic spoons do, indeed, use one helluva lot of them; therefore the higher count would not effect any disadvantage. As a matter of fact—the user could actually get additional savings in his own handling and storing of the bigger carton.

What do you think? Please, give us the benefit of your comments.

A top executive's idea about ideas—sent along to a subordinate manager who, he feels, values action more than thinking.

Let's agree that in this company the ability to produce an idea is one of the most outstanding skills. And let's agree that to produce an original, practical, profitable idea is the greatest possible contribution, deserving of the highest reward a grateful management can devise.

A memo sent from the vice-president, personnel, to the president and other vice-presidents of a company pointing up the implications of employee involvement in a company event. The writer uses the event to say something about employees that sounds very much like industrial psychologist Douglas McGregor's Theory Y concept concerning the devotion of people to work—an idea that might reorient the company's thinking about basic personnel policy.

I am not certain whether this message is about an event—Family Day—or about people—those who worked so hard—or about us and whether we are really fulfilling our job as managers.

I can best attempt to get my thoughts across by talking about Family Day and the thought processes that led me to send this note.

Family Day seemed to be a resounding success—but that is not the point. I won't even discuss the efforts put into its preparation for the past few months, for much of that was done as part of our people's regular day's work. But I'd like to talk more about the people involved and the implication of their efforts. All during last week people in the office and the plant were meeting and working during and after work hours to tie up all the details of the event. On Saturday there were twenty or thirty people here working (mostly on their own time) from early morning until at least 3:45 P.M. that I'm aware of. And then on Sunday there were these same people plus many, many more working for no pay and very little glory from early in the morning until who knows how late (there were still a couple of dozen here when I left at 7:30). And when I say working, I mean tiring physical work.

I was struck, as I drove home and reflected on the day, by the fact that some of these people were the same individuals whom I have heard maligned either as individuals or as a group as "having nothing to do" or "possessing no sense of urgency." The obvious point struck me. They do care. They do have a sense of urgency. And they are capable of expansive quantities of work—if they are given a chance, reason, and support; if they can see a purpose for their work; if they can receive the proper reward (psychological in this case).

This, then, is why I say we should look very closely to ourselves when we criticize *any* part of our organization, before we quickly palm off our occasional ills as being "their" fault. We sure as hell should look hard at whether we are really providing the climate, reasons, and rewards for people to want to work to their fullest capacity.

INFORMATION   (FYI)

This type of memo aims to inform one or more people of a situation, a development, an achievement—or lack of it. The large number of messages of this kind is suggested by the use of the FYI acronym—**F**or **Y**our **I**nformation. Sometimes an information memo is intended as a basis for a subsequent action. In any case, a special requirement is specificity of detail. Occasionally, a memo intended to tell all raises questions by ambiguity or lack of clarity. Frequently, an information memo is sent as a reply to a memo of inquiry.

Style of presentation is of special importance: a key piece of information buried in a flood of words may well go unnoticed. Accordingly, organization on the page, underlining, separation of sentences or paragraphs so that content stands out clearly, all sharpen the effectiveness of the message. The use of visual material—charts, graphs, numerical data—is also helpful.

General manager of a plastics-fabricating firm tells his production staff of a current supply situation. This is clearly essential information for managers to have, in order to operate intelligently under the circumstances described. Too often top management assumes lower-echelon managers somehow know about situations like this, or, even worse, don't need to know.

There is now a critical resin shortage developing. We think it advisable that you be informed and knowledgeable in this matter for the benefit of your field salesmen and their customers.

This company is one of the country's largest volume consumers of resins. As the shortages develop further our leadership position will probably insure our high priority of supply. It may be that the smaller volume users (our price-cutting competitors) could be caught in that proverbial crunch of raw-material shortage and accompanying price increases.

There is currently a growing demand for plastics even while there is a world-wide shortage of benzene which is converted to a monomer which is converted to those resins which are used for plastic containers. This condition may not be corrected for a considerable time—measured not in weeks or months but rather in years.

Such a climate naturally causes price increases to flourish both for basic resins and for the converted products. Ours may rapidly become a seller's market! Of course, your Plastics Division will continue to market products to our good customers throughout the country.

A plant manager tells employees the results of a conservation drive—important feedback to justify their efforts and to get cooperation for future programs.

As a result of the recent actions taken at our plant to conform with the president's request to conserve energy, and thanks to your immediate response and cooperation, we are pleased to report the following figures:

	November		
	Last Year	This Year	Reduction
Electric	225,000 KWH	223,000 KWH	2,000 KWH
Oil	4,860 Gal.	4,760 Gal.	100 Gal.
Gas	14,140 Cf.	11,640 Cf.	2,500 Cf.

Your continued help and suggestions for energy-saving methods are most welcome.

Outcome of a "test case" is worth communicating to all, to prevent misunderstandings about similar situations.

We have received word from our insurance company that our policy does not provide health coverage for stepchildren who are not legally adopted. Payments made previously were in error.

Employees with stepchildren who are not adopted are urged to obtain coverage through another source as soon as possible as they are not insured under our group policy.

Any questions, contact Janice Kelly in Personnel.

Explanation for a new company rule—a good way to get compliance.

Reason for the No Smoking signs posted in the yard is that flammable materials are now being stored in the adjoining shed. Please avoid accidents by obeying the warning signs.

From the president of a company to his management staff. The purpose is to make the staff aware of the current state of the company. Such an overview is a good way to get all echelons below the top familiar with and sympathetic to company goals and actions.

The time appears appropriate to share with you and others of our key managerial people my views concerning the problems of our past year and the moves we should take to insure the future growth that we are all looking forward to.

We all recognize that this past year resulted in one of our poorest periods in terms of financial return. (I emphasize that it was a poor year in *our* terms; for it is certainly true that in our current national economic position many companies would have been delighted to exchange "statements" with us).

. . . paragraph 2 shows how a dismal fact can be made to show a brighter side.

We further recognize that this downtrend occurred in a year where many of our key people expended greater personal effort than ever before. Consequently, we'd like to review some of the principal reasons for our company's less than desirable performance.

The major areas which contributed to our recent situation have been multifold: increased warehousing costs, cost of carrying excessive inventory, increase in overhead, personnel payroll, increased labor and benefit costs, significant start-up costs. sizable back royalty payments, less than estimated sales increases in plastics, etc.

Hopefully, we will not have in this upcoming year any "one-time costs" of the magnitude of those we experienced this past year.

. . . a positive gung-ho note is sounded.

Of importance now is for you to know that the management of your company is committed to maintaining and increasing its position as the leader in its industry. In order to do this in the face of ever increasing competition we must be the most innovative and efficient company in the industry. We have been before and we will be again.

. . . a reasonable pull-up-your-socks request.
A review of this memo will show that a gloomy set of facts has been presented with minimum threat and a good chance of getting strong support.

My request to you is that you address yourself to an immediate effort to "tighten up" those areas over which you have control.

Thanks for your time in reviewing this letter and please feel free to contact me if you have any specific thoughts you would like to share.

There's a new company transportation service.

This is to inform all employees that starting Monday, May 22, we will have a regular company bus service from the railroad station in White Plains to the plant, at 15-minute intervals:

Leaving the station: 8:20; 8:35; 8:50.

The return trips, pickup in front of the administration building:

Leaving company premises: 4:35; 4:50; 5:05.

See your supervisor if there is any problem in connection with these schedules.

Head of a committee to plan an off-premises staff conference writes to the participants about recreation opportunities. The kidding note undoubtedly humanizes the company to employees.

While I appreciate that each of you is task- and goals-oriented, and identifies overwhelmingly with corporate objectives, still I must urge you to think about taking time off from regular duties while at Gurney's—refresh the spirit, recharge the batteries, all that sort of thing.

Consequently, on Friday afternoon, there will be placed at your disposal more than four hours in which you will be free to do your thing. There will be:

• Golf—group rate is approximately $10 per player. Golf and pull carts available. Golf rental sets, $5.

• Tennis (tennis togs required)—$6 per person (unlimited play).

• Horseback riding—$6 per hour.

• Charter boat—$120 for six persons for half day, fee includes bait, tackle, and tip to mate.

• There will also be bikes and boats for sailing. I can't specify the fees at this time.

• Ping-Pong, pool, and other indoor sports. Enjoy!

INQUIRY

A message that raises a question and asks for a reply is an essential communications link. Just consider how helpful a memo of inquiry can be:

• *It can prevent unnecessary activity.* For example, an executive writes, "Would you be interested in an analysis of last quarter's activity of Product X?" If the boss says no, a lot of unwanted and unnecessary work will not be done.

• *It can supply a missing key.* An inquiry can elicit a piece of information needed to resolve a problem.

The memo of inquiry may raise questions of timing, mood, situation, and so on, as well as matters of simple fact.

Message handwritten over a typed proposal taken from a manager's tickler file and sent to the sender. The proposal had to do with a new-product development idea.

Any action here?

A salesman writes a home-office sales manager about an apparent error in a sales tool.

My new "Information Handbook" has the following in the index: Customer Service, pages 54–62.

The pages referred to are about making cold calls. Did I get an imperfect copy? Let me know.

This memo is the reply to the query above.

A mistake was made in printing the Handbook. The correct pages for Customer Service are 102 and 108. Please make the change. We'll correct the error in the next version and notify the field in the newsletter. Thanks for calling our attention to the mixup.

This handwritten note was sent to a colleague who had encouraged the writer to spend an extra weekend at a resort hotel that had been the scene of a business meeting: "The company'll pick up the tab." The message was written over a form from the treasurer's office stating that the weekend costs were considered a personal expense.

Now what the hell do I do?

A production executive of an office-supply firm asks the promotion manager for specific feedback.

It would be helpful to Production to learn the results of various promotions which you inaugurate. In some cases this may mean direct feedback to a manager who has worked on a specific product. Specifically, it would be helpful for us to know:

1. How did the salesmen respond to the product information material we developed for them?

2. How successful was our exhibit in the business show?

3. How are the preliminary reactions to the new desktop line?

. . . numbering specific questions is a good way to clarify what's wanted, and makes it more likely you'll get what you want.

No question of remissness here, Ed, as you're one of the best memoers in the business. Answers to the above may actually duplicate information already sent. At any rate, I'd appreciate having the answers to the above.

A manager raises a question with the personnel department. Notice how the last two words add urgency.

The antidiscrimination regulations are obviously going to put pressure on many firms, including ours, to equip women, among other groups, to rise to management ranks. Is there something we should be doing in the training area for our secretaries? I realize this is a hell

of a bigger question than the few words suggest
But should we be discussing it? And soon?

INSTRUCTIONS *See* Orders and Instructions

INVITATIONS

Usually, you send this type of message because you want some individual or group to be present at a particular time and place. But there's another less literal form that comes under this heading: You "invite" a person to do something; a courteous approach to getting action.

Head of an informal gourmet club sends out an announcement.

Dear Bouillabaisseurs et Paellaistos:
Can we make another tentative date for a financially lunatic, but gastronomically triumphant, ritual lunch next Friday?
Barbara Williams is hereby nominated to select a theme dish and a target restaurant. Okay, all around? Signify by giving the secret sign to Gene Miller, our Roundup Director.

Open house on the company premises. The "surprise guest" is the company founder, recently retired. Whether or not this type of invitation is a command performance is largely a matter of company tradition. For the most part, firms try to make these affairs so attractive that those who don't attend regret it. Of course, if employees are reluctant to attend, the affair probably shouldn't be given.

You and your families are invited to Company Day Anniversary, to take place in our own dining-room area on Saturday afternoon at 2:00 P.M.
This year we celebrate our 28th anniversary, and the Committee has labored hard and long to make it a pleasant and memorable event.
Food and drink for every taste will be provided. You'll be entertained by a short but exciting program, *featuring a surprise guest.*
As usual, there will be tours of the plant and offices for all those interested. Come and meet old friends, and help honor the occasion!

"Join our informal work discussion group."

A group of us are getting together, perhaps on a biweekly basis—to be decided later—for informal discussions of work problems or anything else that may develop. If you'd like to join us, we've reserved a table for lunch at Tony's for 12:30 next Tuesday.

A vice-president invites his staff and friends of the "anniversarian" to a celebration.

You are cordially invited to join me for a drink tomorrow afternoon, October 17, at 4:30 in my office to help celebrate Bert Feld's 20th anniversary with the company.

I hope you can join us.

This is an example of the "invitation to take action" type of memo.

You've just concluded your fifth year as supervisor with our company! Congratulations! We hope time hasn't hung heavy. This is to remind you that you now qualify for our Management Club, and the officers would be pleased to receive an application for membership from you.

"I TOLD YOU SO"

Every once in a while an executive is lucky—he thinks. Something has happened that he predicted. An action was taken that he warned against and, happy day, he has been right!

It's always nice to have one's views reinforced. But the "I told you so" memo is usually written by that not altogether admirable person, the poor winner. However, in certain situations the "I told you so" memo can avoid the crowing and the implied rebuke it suggests. Here are some samples that almost make the message palatable.

A superior to a subordinate; the moderate tone and constructive conclusion take the curse off the fault-finding.

Just got the production figures for last month, and although they're better than the previous period, they fall substantially short of target.

You'll remember that we discussed the departmental situation and contrary to my expectations, you were certain that goals would be met. The reason for optimism seemed to be that you and your people would bear down, push hard to get over the line.

Now I'm sure there was no lack of effort. More than ever, I'm convinced that what's needed is an overhaul of the entire operation—everything from more careful work planning to better utilization of your people.

I realize it's a big job, but when the old ways don't work, new methods must be developed. I'll be glad to sit down with you and map out an approach that could brighten the production picture for the future.

When this type of message goes from a subordinate to his boss, the writing problem becomes more ticklish. Here a head-on but humorous approach may just do it. Clearly, the two have a good rapport.

Hear that Steve Avery quit last week. I hate to say, "I told you so," but I did, didn't I? You'll never get me to admit I'm smarter than you are, but I did have a chance to see Avery operate at a closer vantage point. If you promise not to hold it against me, I'll try to continue to be right in the future, particularly when you ask for my opinion.

Here the writer and recipient are at the same organizational level. "Y-ness" refers to industrial psychologist Douglas McGregor's idea that most people are willing to accept responsibility and work on their own initiative when given the chance.

Never mind the ten bucks you owe me. If your conscience hurts, you can buy me a lunch some day. Bet aside, the important thing is that my faith in the Smith-Calvison team paid off. Actually, I was betting on the ability of those two people to respond to a clear-cut challenge, on their own. Everything I believe about the "Y-ness" of human beings was at stake. I'm hoping that aside from a temporary partisanship, you're as pleased as I am at the successful outcome.

"I WAS WRONG" (*see also* Apology *and* "You Were Right")

Clearly this type of memo is the opposite of the preceding "I told you so" variety. The "I was wrong" theme can do good for two people, the sender and the receiver. In some cases it can be a generous acknowledgment that someone else was right. When properly written, this message also, as confession is supposed to do, improves the state of one's soul. Of almost equal importance, it can also save face.

Although closely related to the Apology, there is a difference in tone. An apology expresses regret, contrition. One can be wrong without necessarily being sorry.

"I didn't guess right on our quitting-time experiment."

The evaluation session yesterday on our staggered quitting time arrangement seems to show that it's working, despite the doubts I initially expressed. Well, smarter people than I have been caught with their predictions down! Since you were the original advocate of the idea, congratulations are in order. Shows that a man of strong conviction can win out against us dullards!

The writer admits to a mistake in meeting tactics.

Put it down to exasperation, Boss. After it was over—as a matter of fact, halfway through the hassle—I realized it was stupid to take up the group's time trying to crack that old chestnut with Paul. I guess we'll always disagree about how to handle the red-tape problem. But that was no excuse for upsetting the meeting on a subject that at best was only vaguely related to the main subject. It won't happen again.

"Pardon my bad manners."

My good intentions aside, I didn't mean to contradict you in the presence of your secretary. Although it may not have seemed so, I was trying to help. Perhaps when there's less pressure on us, we should get C. R. to give us his views on the subject. Please tell Hazel I regret my bad manners.

A production engineer goes way out on a limb with a customer—and tries to minimize the damage.

We've all had the experience of starting to do something, realizing it's wrong, and yet we continue on, and on, and on. . . . That's the nightmarish feeling I had halfway through my conversation with Gordon Abel of Connerly products. I know you sent me down there just to check our installation. But I found myself making claims and promising guaranteed performance that our salesman never would duplicate. Put it down to overeagerness to please, or temporary insanity.

Anyhow—my mistake should be rectified. I'll be willing (not glad) to contact Abel and try as diplomatically as possible to undo the damage. But perhaps Jim Lesser, who has the account, would rather handle it.

You make the decision, or let's discuss the situation further, if you think I can clarify it more.

"I'm wrong, but I feel right."

I was wrong about the Hartdale account, and I see they've just canceled. Well, I don't believe the customer is always right, and this is one case where I'd rather be wrong than president. We can go just so far in satisfying customer demands. Past that point, we're overindulging a customer and weakening the integrity of our position.

I believe that if we continue to be wrong in the way I seem to have been, we'll be better off for it in the long run.

"LET'S DISCUSS"

A problem may arise that requires an exchange of views. The memo writer describes the situation and suggests a meeting or some action to deal with it. The simplest form of the message merely raises the question at issue. Also included may be a rundown of aspects of the problem to be touched on—an agenda, as it were—and suggestions for a meeting—when, where, and so on.

A movie producer sends a memo to his director about a work problem (in connection with Gone With the Wind*).*

To: Mr. Cukor   December 8, 1938

For your information, I am informed by MGM that Clark Gable refuses under any circumstances to have any kind of a Southern accent.

I am very anxious to talk to you generally

about this entire accent problem, and would appreciate it if you would make a note to take it up with me when you see me tomorrow.

DOS
Memo From David O. Selznick

We're going to be working together, so let's talk.

Just got a note from Bill Devaney that he'd like you and me to develop some new-product ideas and work together as a two-man team. Fine with me. As a matter of fact, I'm strongly hopeful that this will be a case where two heads will not only be better than one but even better than two working independently.

Let's get together as soon as possible and make plans that will optimize the opportunities.

The writer asks for a meeting to clear up the fog around a new procedure.

I've read and reread your memo about the new procedure for customer contacts. I must confess quite simply that I don't understand what's intended. Perhaps the wisest thing to do at this point is to get together and iron out the details. When would be a convenient time for you?

The advent of a new secretary, to be shared by two executives, gets one to write to the other to suggest a planning session.

I understand from Dell Bertram that the new secretary is due to report next Monday. To avoid misunderstanding and confusion, don't you think we'd better straighten out in advance just how her time should be allocated? How about right after lunch on Thursday?

MEETINGS, AGENDAS

Meetings come in all shapes and sizes, from a two-person get-together to the large-group conference. If you run a meeting, you know that it helps to plan the points to be covered. It helps even further to announce the subject matter to the participants in advance. People like to pre-think a subject, or organize their thoughts on a matter coming up for discussion.

Effective executives routinely send out brief outlines or agendas of their meetings.

Or they specify the preparations to be made—information to bring, reports to have available, areas on which to bone up. To avoid having an announced agenda sound cut-and-dried, flexibility can be added by a final item like ". . . and any other relevant matters that are brought up" or suggesting that the items listed are only a partial coverage.

There's another point to be made about memos announcing a meeting and that is the relationship between the actual planning and what's to be included in the memo. For example, you may plan your meeting in some detail but only wish to announce the broad subject to be discussed. Or you may want to provide the details, including specified contributions expected from various participants.

Summaries of meetings, or meeting follow-ups will be found under the Meetings, Recaps heading.

One-point agenda for a small meeting.

Can we get together to discuss the production schedule for the next month? Remember, two new developments will have to be worked around: the #6 press is down and won't be available until the 15th; and, as of this moment, Purchasing hasn't been able to get any .125 sheet stock. How about Tuesday at three, in your office?

Short and sweet.

There will be a meeting in the conference room at 9:30 Monday morning, April 8, at which Mr. Reed will explain the new major medical plan.

A department head reschedules a staff meeting.

The regular staff meeting scheduled for Friday afternoon will have to be canceled because of a conflict with front office matters. Instead, we'll have a catch-up meeting Monday at 10:00. Of course, I'll be available to take up any urgent business that can't wait until our get-together.

Reminder: Sally is to give a brief rundown of her visit to the Washington office. Hal is to review his recent customer contact experience.

A sales manager to the head of sales about his idea for a meeting agenda.

Thanks for giving me a chance to vote on the kind of agenda I'd like to see at our next regional sales meeting:

I'm against *inflated* agendas.

I'm against *deflated* agendas.

I'm for *flated* agendas—those that take up a reasonable number of our most pressing concerns, allowing enough time to cover each within our given time limits.

If you like, I'll spell out what I have in mind next time we get together.

Here is an agenda of a meeting of supervisors in the company's main location. The agenda has been kept loose and general, to give the conference leader freedom to move in fruitful directions as they grow out of the discussion.

Supervisory Conference
Tentative Schedule and Agenda

Subject: Today's Operating Problems—and Opportunities

9:15 Check in at reception desk, Administration Building

9:20 Coffee in conference room

9:45 Welcome to Headquarters by James May
Statement of the conference theme by Les Raymond

Importance of the subject

Identify problem areas

Pinning down the relevant problems to the departments concerned

10:45 Coffee break

11:00 Further problem identification and refinement

12:00 Lunch

12:45 Trouble factors: Circumstances that create management headaches

Solutions to the problems

Converting problems into opportunities

2:45 Coffee break

3:00 General discussion

4:00 Conference adjourns—James May

A department head sets up a meeting with the head of an adjoining unit, to which each will bring two or three subordinates.

Here's a rundown of subjects we should discuss at our meeting next Thursday:

1. Ideas for a replacement of the shelves now being used in Storage Room C (we both agree

they're past the repair stage). What will be the timetable for doing this?

2. Can we organize a joint Safety and Housekeeping Committee, with equal representation from both departments? Who? How many? When? And how will it operate?

3. There's been a certain amount of conflict in materials delivery, especially when large orders are going through the departments at the same time. What can we do to minimize this problem?

We should probably also discuss other ways and means for keeping up cooperation between the two departments, improving attitudes between our workgroups—that is, making them friendlier.

Have I forgotten anything? See you Thursday.

MEETINGS, RECAPS

There's an old joke around that news events don't *really* happen unless they've been reported in *The New York Times.* What actually took place at a meeting or related type of event may not jell even *after* the event unless it's been put down on paper. That's the purpose of the memos under this heading.

One manager sums up the agreements made in an earlier discussion.

Here is my understanding of what we agreed to this morning:

1. We will no longer use the room next to the cafeteria for storage.

2. You and I will both go through the storage area, removing or labeling for removal items that we want to retain.

3. Maintenance will then clean out whatever is left.

4. The use of the room will then revert to the people running the cafeteria.

Sounds simple now that I've put it down on paper, but it took hours of talking to get there.

But you know, I don't think we could have reached agreement in less time.

A production executive recaps a meeting with a sales executive that had the purpose of setting up an agenda for a larger subsequent meeting.

To tie down the things we discussed in our talk this morning:
• My group will meet with you in the conference room on Wednesday, November 20, at 9:30.
• We will talk about setting up customer-location visits of production people with our field representatives.
• Also on the agenda: other ways and means that sales and production can assist one another.
• Any matters of interest that any of us comes up with.
It would be helpful if early in the meeting you give us a brief fill-in on sales planning for the next quarter.
Look forward to our get-together.

A production executive arranges for follow-up of a meeting he's had with one of his foremen.

So that we can optimize the follow-up of our meeting, here's a recap of the action points:
You are to get together the figures on rework, rejects, etc., in your department for the last two months.
I am to ask the Cost Department to determine what downtime on an injection press comes to. We both understand this will have to be very rough, but we'll try for some ballpark figure.
I'm to talk to Production Control to see what can be done to equalize the work flow into your department.
You're to talk to Mark Berry to see about a personnel-exchange plan to take care of major idle time.
I'm very pleased with the outcome of our talk. I hope you are. There's bound to be a good result from the digging we've done.

A recap, along with a call for the next step.

That was a very worthwhile discussion we had. Let's make sure to parlay our accomplish-

162

ments by putting a lot of muscle in the follow-up. We were awfully good at expressing our intentions. Now let's push for the payoff by action.

Thinking over our meeting this morning, I feel even more strongly that we must cut down on the size of the group. Unfortunately, the drawbacks and losses don't show on the surface. Matters go along evenly enough, thanks to your skillful handling. But that very smoothness covers over the fact that many people are not participating —John and Dora, for example, haven't opened their mouths in the past two sessions.

And discussions really don't get down to the nitty gritty. Some people hesitate to be as blunt and direct as they might in a smaller group. And others, aware that more people want to speak up on a point, cut down on the length of their own remarks.

How about splitting the group into three units of six people each, and establishing some kind of interface among the three? I know this creates other kinds of problems—but at this point, I'm in favor of changing the problem. My feeling is, there will be a net gain.

A conferee reports his impression to the manager who ran the meeting.

Great meeting, Tom! Thanks to your planning, enthusiasm couldn't have gone any higher without the group tearing down the building posts. Thought you'd like some feedback.

NEGOTIATION

Ongoing matters require discussion, comment, plan-making, seeking of agreement, and so on. Although this type of communication is usually best made face to face, there are occasions when the written word must be used. If you find yourself composing a memo of this kind and getting bogged down, the simplest solution may be to pick up the phone or write a memo suggesting a get-together. However, the examples here show some of the requirements and approaches of this subject.

A manager offers a plan for the emptying out of a shared storage space.

As you know, our use of the warehouse near Building B is decidedly unbalanced. Your stuff takes up all of one floor, we've used only about half of the basement. However, to get the cleaning-out process going (and eventually completed) I'm willing to send my people over for about 10-man-days a week. I put it on this basis rather than saying two men a day for five days because I'd use that operation as fill-in for people between regular assignments. Two things: you supply the supervisor, and your group is to put in about twice as many man-hours as we do.

I hope you agree this is fair. Let me know your reaction.

Transferring employees between departments to even workloads is common practice. Shortages make it even more common—and arrangements must be made.

H. B. suggests that you and I get together on a method of swapping people. I don't know about you, but the delivery of sheet stock we use for assemblies is erratic, and sometimes I have as many as ten machine operators standing around. We'll have to move on a short-notice basis because right now I don't know where we stand from day to day.

According to H. B., your molding powder situation is a little more stable, but last week he said you had to shut down three machines.

Of course, we've got to settle pay rates and tell the people what's going on, and get their agreement.

Let's get together Tuesday—time to be arranged—and clean up the details.

The days of barter are not altogether gone.

Would you be interested in swapping three 5-drawer file cabinets in return for three 4-drawers? I need more filing space, and perhaps you're not using what you've got.

As you know, the screws are tightening on purchases. Advantages to you in this deal are that my cabinets are newer and you'd be doing that great thing called cooperating!

Tussle over a valued employee.

Mr. Ball tells me you've got a job opening that would be a step up for Connie Harris. Further, Connie tells me you've approached her. I think that's lousy management practice, to talk to her without checking with me first.

Connie's got as good a future in my unit as she'd have in yours. I'm telling this to Mr. Ball.

Connie herself wants to stay. However, I'm open to persuasion. If you can show me that she's really got something to gain, I won't stand in her way—if she wants out.

From a sales executive to a psychologist-consultant who is to design a survey for the firm.

Thank you very much for your note of December 1 and the attached outline of your survey. I feel that we are in close agreement on our approach to this matter.

I am enclosing a group of questions which we are considering. These of course are still very rough, not in shape for tabulating, and out of order.

This is going to be a difficult survey to design, because we will have to start off with a number of qualifying questions (i.e., Do you employ women on your sales force?) and then direct the reader to branch off according to the reply. We also feel that we must design questions for saleswomen (after securing their names and addresses from the first survey).

We are working on this design now and will be glad to meet with you to discuss it at any time. I suggest that perhaps the best time would be after we have developed a first draft.

Please let me know your reaction to this, and don't hesitate to telephone me at any time. We are all looking forward to the pleasure of meeting you.

ORDERS AND INSTRUCTIONS

"Do this," "Do that," "Come here," "Go there," "See X," "See Y,"—on the workscene there is almost no end to instructions. To a large extent orders are verbal. There's no need to put down on paper such statements as, "Please ask Mr. Smith for the Acme file" or "Please order a ham sandwich for my lunch."

But there are often good reasons for orders and instructions to take the written form. For example, when the task to be performed is complicated; when there are many details; when there are cautions and qualifications; when it's desirable to add graphic material—sketches, charts, etc.

Semantically there is a distinction between orders and instructions. The former suggests a simple command. Instructions may be a series of statements that clarify *what's* to be done, *where* it's to be done, *when* it's to be done, *how* it's to be done, and sometimes even *why* it's to be done. As will be noted in the samples, the tone of an order may vary from a flat-out command to what seems to be almost a request for cooperation or compliance. But the intention is always the same: There's something to be done and the recipient of the memo is to do it.

The request form of order.

Don't you think it would be a good idea for you to stay close to the new expediter, especially for the first two weeks, until he gets the hang of things? Remember, his experience isn't too heavy, and he seems to have enough on the ball to warrant the investment of time.

Velvet glove, iron hand.

I'd like to see the corridor in your department cleaned up by next Friday and kept free of litter and mess thereafter.

Flat order.

I expect all departmental production reports on my desk each morning before noon. Thank you.

This memo makes the point that when one speaks with authority, an order can be low pressured indeed. This top executive is saying, "Be there!" The quiet tone doesn't belie the order's need-to-obey.

Will you and your staff meet with me briefly in the conference room at 9 A.M. on Wednesday to discuss our compliance with the antidiscrimination laws?

To a secretary from a boss who's going to be out for a couple of weeks. The detail supplied is in the form of a mini work schedule.

Please make a note on your calendar to take care of the following matters as they fall due:

1. *Monday, January 25.* Responses should start trickling in to the customer survey which was mailed on January 20. Please tabulate these by industry and company size and hold until my return.

2. *Friday, January 29.* See that Mae G. gets a copy of the monthly sales report so that she can make any necessary corrections.

3. *Monday, February 3.* Hal Blair has promised to deliver copy on the pollution report. Please make necessary copies and give one to Hadway, together with a copy of the previous one, so he can begin to familiarize himself with the project.

4. *Wednesday, February 5.* Dora Melson is working on a report on marketing strategy. In case she should need the names of typical customers, please ask Ed Jones if he could supply some. If possible, I would like to see a rough draft of this report by the time I return.

The vacation-bound executive who wrote the previous memo to his secretary covers himself up the line. "What," you may say, "give instructions to one's boss?" Here's an instance where it's appropriate—if properly done.

I am attaching a copy of a memo to Grace which summarizes the status of work in progress. I don't expect that there will be any problems with any of these items, since they are now in her good hands.

One thing you might want to keep an eye on is Dora Melson's report. I'm counting on Ed Jones to come through with the names of typical customers, should they be needed. If there's any problem in this area, will you please expedite?

An afterthought: if you want to have an early meeting on the customer-survey tabulations, please include Dave Momsen in the discussion, since he'll be working on the interpretations later on.

ORIENTATION

When a new employee is introduced into unfamiliar surroundings, it is helpful for him to be told enough about his situation to:
- Have it seem less unfamiliar
- Minimize the chances for accident, error, or mishap
- Shorten the period of strangeness and hasten the time when he can function effectively in the new situation

Usually these objectives are achieved through company brochures and in face-to-face conversation—with an immediate superior, co-workers, and so on. But a memo can reinforce other contacts, and it makes messages possible from those who ordinarily may not see the new employee.

A company president greets a new middle-management employee.

Just a brief note which I'll be following up in person as soon as I get back from the Coast. But I want you to know how pleased we all are that you've joined us. I know this will be a rewarding association for all concerned. Meanwhile, be assured of my very best wishes for a fulfilling future.

A note sent to a technician makes its point because of its directness and simplicity.

Our personnel director, Mr. Brody, has told me that you'll be starting in the Standards Department on Monday, February 25. Jay Wootten, the department head, is a most capable manager, and I'm sure you'll enjoy your association with him. Our company has a reputation for being a good place to work. I hope you'll find it so—and then some.

A general foreman posts a notice on the bulletin board. Purpose is to show

On March 1 Miss Helen Lember will be joining the department to assume duties as an assistant *management's full backing for an innovation—a female operator on the giant mixing rolls.*

rollroom operator. Miss Lember has been with the company for five years, serving in the Inspection Department, where she turned in an outstanding record. I'm sure we'll all do what we can to welcome her to her new job, and to help her feel at home in true company spirit.

The young shipping clerk who received this message had it framed and hung in his kitchen.

Welcome to the R. L. Flood Company. I personally hope you'll like working here, and that you'll come to enjoy your association with the fine men and women who are your colleagues.

Ours is not a very old company—we'll reach our eighteenth year this November—but we've established a reputation for a good product and a harmonious and dedicated group of employees.

I'm fortunate to be the founder of this organization, but you can be sure that it's been the effort and creativity of our employees at every level—people like you yourself—who have made our good name.

I hope you will spend many rewarding years with us.

PERMISSION

See Authorization

PERSUASION

(*see also* Ideas; Proposals; *and* Suggestions)

Offhand one might think that persuasion is very much a word-of-mouth operation. It would seem that as is true of much salesmanship, it's necessary to give the persuadee the opportunity to raise objections which then can be overcome. However, the effectiveness of direct mail selling, in which millions of dollars worth of goods is moved entirely by the printed word, demonstrates that it's possible to get someone to do something by words on paper that perhaps he might otherwise ignore or resist.

An executive assistant tries to get his boss to reconsider a decision.

I know you've always taken a dim view of off-premises staff meetings. And certainly, the objections you've raised are completely valid: Yes, it's possible that the surroundings may water down the business purposes; yes, partying can get out of hand; yes, part-time athletes may come limping into the conference room with aches and pains that make concentration difficult.

In general I share your feelings. But our next meeting seems to have special requirements. I think our group is in the doldrums. We've been working in a negative, depressed climate for some time and to clear the air and shake things up in a constructive way, we have to do something new and different. I'm not saying that a meeting at some out-of-town hotel is the answer to our ills, but it *is* a way of dramatizing the fact that we're capable of change, that we are, indeed, making one.

In brief, I feel that an off-premises conference has advantages now that are important to us. Won't you please reconsider this matter in light of the above?

Training director asks his boss, the company president, to kick off the first of a series of supervisory meetings.

Our first meeting of the supervisory group is scheduled for the first Tuesday in March, at 5:30 in the cafeteria. I know better than most how pressed you are for time, but nevertheless I'd like to ask you to officiate at the opening session.

These meetings need all the boost they can get. Your presence will show, as nothing else could, that top management is behind the program. And your personal popularity is sure to get us off with a bang.

Specifically, what I have in mind is an agenda along these lines: I would introduce you, then you open the meeting with a speech on the aims and importance of our management-training program—about 15–20 minutes.

You can feel free to leave after turning the floor over to me. The balance of the meeting will be devoted to problem identification—giving the supervisors an opportunity to spell out their ideas.

Total time required on your part, from 5:20 to about 6. I hope you agree that it would be a worthwhile time investment.

Another version of the same message as that above.

I'd like to start our meeting series with a strong opener—namely, you! A kickoff talk, to run fifteen minutes, about the aims of our training program should do it. Date is the first Tuesday in March. How about it?

From a vice-president, personnel, to the head of a production taskforce who seems to be too good an employee to lose.

I've just been told that you're considering leaving the company for what's been described to me as "a job with better opportunity." You know we're good enough friends for me to wish you well. And I wouldn't want to do anything to interfere with your personal progress. But I do have some idea of your abilities and how they could be used in this company. It's my feeling that unless the new opportunity is vastly greater than your present situation you might do well to look around here for possibilities to explore. It's true, you probably haven't gotten the full recognition you deserve. Few of us do. But I'm sure if you review your prospects with your superior, he'll be able to suggest a potential here that might give more of the things you want in a career than you could, for sure, find in any other organization. I'd be glad to discuss this important matter with you further.

Not a memo, strictly speaking, but an advertisement run over the name of Governor Thomas J. Meskill of Connecticut. However, the elements of persuasion are well illustrated, especially the pinpointing of the benefits *of what's advocated, that being, "Set up your business in Connecticut."*

Busy executives have two kinds of problems— the ones they have been handling in day-to-day management, and the special ones that are coming in the years ahead.

A Connecticut location can help solve many of the routine problems so that executive talent can concentrate on managing the new pressures:

• PEOPLE. Plenty of good people, technically

trained for business and industry. Skilled workers, excellent office personnel.

• TAXES. Connecticut has absolutely no state or local personal income tax—is lowering the cost of doing business through other tax reductions.

• MONEY. Long-term, low-cost revenue bond financing (6½% average so far) for all forms of business and industrial development—including pollution control.

• MARKETS. An overnight truck market of 54 million customers. Convenient, modern highway, rail, air and marine facilities to speed people and products around the world.

• LOCATIONS. Scores of cooperative, easy-to-reach communities with prime space for every type of economic development. Public services to assure you and your company a high degree of safety and security.

• SERVICES. A newly formed State Department of Commerce to provide tailor-made help with site locations, development technology, international trade and marine commerce.

• LIFESTYLE. The nation's finest. Residential, recreational, educational and cultural resources that attract the management on whom company futures depend, that provide an enriched family life. And because commuting time is sharply reduced, there's more of life to spend as a family.

Relocating your company to Connecticut may not solve all executive problems. But we'll give you more help than anybody else we know. (As we did for G.E., American Can, GT&E, Uniroyal, Xerox and dozens of others).

And we'll provide you and your people with a better, richer, fuller, longer, more productive life in the bargain.

POINTING WITH PRIDE

The politician is a professional who typically "points with pride" and, oppositely, "views with alarm." Since business executives often emulate their opposite numbers in the field of politics, both these devices will be found here (for Viewing with Alarm, see page 223).

Pointing with Pride requires two things: an event or achievement and an audience that will benefit one way or the other from this activity. One word of caution: Make sure that the event is worthy of the effort and the audience is likely to be properly impressed.

A manager drops a line to the president of the company about the meritorious service of three subordinates.

Delighted to hear about the big order we landed with American on the new line. While I'm sure Sales deserves major credit, I feel some recognition should also go to the production supervisors who spent considerable time despite their pressing duties in helping work out the production procedures and costs that eventually figured in the proposals made to the customer.

Three supervisors, namely, Ted Mann, Leo Margolis, and Les Kelly, did a particularly good job, and I believe would appreciate some acknowledgment of their contribution.

From the production manager to the safety engineer, giving credit to properly prepared employees for deft handling of an emergency.

The fire that broke out in the Assembly Department could have been serious. It was the coolheadedness of the employees that accounted for the fast action that led to the quick dousing of the flames. And their behavior, in turn, was the result of our continuing safety program that gave them both the training and the knowledge they needed to handle the firefighting equipment safely.

Score a home run for safety education!

A manager points to handmade Christmas decorations as a sign of employee creativity.

I know you're very busy, particularly as we head into the new year, but if you should have a few minutes, particularly while you're in the plant, I think you'd be pleased at what you'd find in the Shipping Room. The people there on their own initiative have put out Christmas decorations for the holiday. These are not bought items but for the most part decorations they've made themselves. I think you'd get a boost out of seeing how creative our people can be.

Head of a hand-tool manufacturer's service department writes to the vice-president of marketing about an outstanding selling job.

October 15   Ed Greene, one of our service engineers, calls on Raleigh Tool Co. on a routine visit. He learns that the company has recently gotten a new purchasing executive. On his return, Greene passes this information to Pete Vance, of Sales.

October 22   Vance tells Bob Grinzer to call on Raleigh to present our new line of small power tools.

November 3   Grinzer gives a demonstration of new tools to a group of Raleigh's production supervisors arranged for by the new purchasing man.

November 18   Grinzer takes a test order for hand drills and sanders.

December 18   Close follow-up by Grinzer leads to quantity orders to the tune of $8,500.

December 25   Merry Christmas to all, thanks to cooperation between Service and Sales.

POLICY ANNOUNCEMENTS

The concepts, rules, and procedures by which a company operates are crucial, not only long-range but also for day-to-day operation. Accordingly, statements about company policy are often critical, and may require special consideration. Clarity of language is not always possible, since meanings may be obscure or ambiguous. At any rate, the writer must make sure that his words represent his precise meaning.

Since policy may become a matter for legal consideration, it may be desirable to have a lawyer take on the responsibility of writing or at least reviewing a given policy statement. As a matter of fact, whenever policy statements involve particular functions—financial, engineering, personnel, and so on—it's a good idea to have the company experts in these specialties either originate or review correspondence in their respective areas.

A treasurer explains a financial situation to operating executives that requires their understanding and cooperation.

Due to the current general economic business atmosphere, we are experiencing a substantial slowdown in collecting monies from our customers. And, we feel strongly that such a serious situation will persist for many months.

To properly finance our planned growth, we have borrowed heavily since the beginning of our new fiscal year. But this general business recession coupled with our company's equipment-purchasing program and inventory buildup and major plant moves, along with big tax payments on the horizon, have put us in an extremely tight cash position.

So that we don't have to borrow additional funds and so that we can properly meet our obligations, we urgently advise you to review all your capital equipment projects for which purchase orders have not been issued. Review each purchase on the basis of a delaying action for as long as possible or an actual canceling of the project at this time. Also, purchase orders which have already been issued for such capital equipment should be carefully reviewed from the standpoint of delaying delivery and, consequently, required payments by us.

Further, all currently authorized expenditures —including the addition of personnel—must be judiciously reviewed. And until further notice, all travel and entertainment should be held to the absolute minimum level.

Our company is now doing very well in both sales gains and profitability! But some of these profits must necessarily be retained in order to pay our current bills. This is just sound fiscal responsibility and we must follow it.

Your good judgment now in this most important and essential matter is required to keep us financially healthy so that we can exploit properly our potential in the immediate and long-term future.

A chemical firm states its stand on the environment issue.

It is the policy of our company to do everything in our power to refrain from adding by one iota to the deterioration of our environment. Accordingly, we appreciate help from any quarter that will make both our operations and our products nonpolluting.

A memo from the labor relations executive to the president and vice-presidents of a company. The intention is to outline the steps that should be taken following an unsuccessful attempt to unionize the firm, in a continuing effort to build employee goodwill.

We recently received an astonishing vote of confidence from the employees of this company. However, underlying this vote was a current of unrest which, if allowed to flow, could in the future inundate our company.

The follow-up of this union campaign can in the long run be as important to us as the campaign itself. My recommendation is that we take the following steps:

1. Personal letter from the president to all hourly employees:

    a. This letter should contain in it the obvious message of appreciation for the confidence placed in the management of this company.

    b. It should also contain an announcement of the president's appointment of a special "task group" panel made up of both hourly and salaried employees whose task it will be to study the results of the upcoming Yale-Laitin survey to make recommendations for the improvement of this company's policies and practices.

2. Letter from the president to all supervisors:

    a. These supervisors were the focal point around which our total campaign was run; and most of them met the challenge with outstanding loyalty and expertise. We must not, at any time, overlook the fact that it was the relationship that has been set up with these foremen that was a critical factor in the winning of this election. This letter should indicate exactly that.

3. Notification to the local newspaper as to the results of the election.

4. Celebration buffet; our NLRB waiting period will be officially over on Monday, November 27.

We will on that day for the full day hold a victory buffet in our cafeteria.

Certainly in the aftermath of this trying election, we do not want to "over-react." But, we must learn from what we have just been through and work with our salaried, supervisory, and hourly employees to make sure that we do not have to go through this again for a long, long while.

Laying it on the line for antidiscrimination.

This company always has treated and will continue to treat all employees with absolute equality, regardless of race, sex, ethnic origin, age, or other personal quality.

PRAISE   (*see also* Advocacy)

Someone has done something, achieved something, been honored. You want to state your pleasure, possibly adding your congratulations.

The complimentary memo gives the manager an opportunity to register his favorable reaction to an event, an accomplishment, and so on.

A complimentary memo is a good way of cementing an old relationship or strengthening a new one. It's your chance to make someone feel good and show that you appreciate an effort. It's the business equivalent of the naval "Well done."

To the recipient a complimentary message means recognition that adds greatly to the psychic reward of achievement. It is a career plus, boosting his ego and fattening his personal file, perhaps providing a help to promotion possibilities in the company. Often as not, the sender gains as much as the receiver, because a common reaction is gratitude and the feeling, "What a nice guy!"

To an employee who just landed a big order.

Think you're pretty hot stuff, don't you? So do I.

Jim Lavenson
President of The Plaza

To the chef who had prepared a magnificent banquet for five hundred dis-

Congratulations, Joe. That was the finest food I've ever tasted. Everyone commented on it. As *criminating guests, the head of the hotel writes . . .*

a matter of fact, only one guest threw up. The one who got the bill.

> Jim Lavenson
> President of the Plaza

A secretary writes to her boss, who has just been made a vice-president of the firm.

No one could be happier—except possibly you yourself—over your promotion. We both know how hard you worked and how much you deserve your new title and responsibilities.

The fact that I'm moving up with you, of course, gives me a selfish reason for being pleased, so—congratulations to the both of us!

An executive writes to a member of his staff on the occasion of his twenty-fifth anniversary with the company.

Twenty-five years—twenty-five great years of creative accomplishment! I've had the benefit of working with you for the last ten years of that period and I want you to know that our association has always been one of the big pluses in my job. So, here's wishing you many more years with a company that has every reason to appreciate your contribution.

The company president sends a message to an employee on his twenty-fifth anniversary.

I will not try an adequate assessment of what your twenty-five years here at Lee & Company have meant to the rest of us. Whatever criterion I apply leads to the conclusion that association with you has enriched all of us, has increased our pleasure and satisfactions and has contributed significantly to making this more the kind of place we would each like it to be.

Please accept my gratitude, and best wishes for a continuing bright future.

From a producer to a movie star—a difficult memo to write, in a milieu where praise is usually overdone.

Mr. Fredric March   April 28, 1937
1026 Ridgedale Drive
Beverly Hills, California

Dear Freddie:

You must have heard from any number of people the most laudatory sort of opinions on your performance in *A Star Is Born.* Yet I fear that many of these statements may have seemed to you automatic flattery of a type you must be used to, and that perhaps you wonder which congratulations are on the level. It is for this reason that I thought I should send you this note to tell you that on all sides I have seldom heard such praise of any actor in any picture. In New York, as here, people are saying that your job is one of the most able and honest that has ever been done for the screen. That it will do a great deal for you, as it has for the picture and therefore for us, is a certainty.

May I add my congratulations (as well as my thanks) to the others? As to whether this is on the level, I remind you of what I told you about certain other performances.

At long last I salute you as I have wanted to through these years, with complete enthusiasm and unstinted admiration. . . .

Yours, etc.,

Memo From David O. Selznick

From a top executive to another who does considerable public speaking and has just addressed a national businessmen's conference.

"Another superb achievement" is the comment one always would like to make of an admired colleague. You create an instance where it applies perfectly. I enjoyed being a witness.

An executive writes to the editor of the company's house organ.

I particularly liked the last issue of the company monthly newspaper. The lead article, on the customer use of our service, was lively and made me feel awfully good about us. And the tribute to George Planter on his retirement said the right things in the right way—real feeling without getting sloppy.

Keep up the good work!

Note written on a report which a boss returns to his subordinate.

Sharp and analytical, bright and imaginative. Damn fine job!

A personnel executive reinforces a supervisor's praise by a note to a rank-and-file employee.

You are working for a hard taskmaster, a man who expects good performance. And you have obviously given him and your company that performance—Jack Lurie's comment on your review form that you are "one of the very best I've ever had work for me" should be a source of real pride.

I sincerely congratulate you for having earned such a fine reputation with Jack.

Keep up the good work.

A letter written by the president of a company to all employees (several hundred) expressing appreciation for their attitudes and performance during a company crisis, a power failure. Spelling out the details of the praised performance adds substance to the message.

I'm taking this somewhat unusual method of talking with you because of an unusual occurrence. Tuesday night at 5:20 your company, along with the rest of New England, fell victim to a massive power failure. What happened here during the next few hours once again impressed me with the caliber of people who make up our company.

When the power failed and the plant plunged into darkness, there was none of the excessive excitement and panic that could have taken place. Foremen, operators, and utility men immediately saw to it that all of the equipment was safely shut off. Employees with flashlights went out to the darkened areas of the plant to act as guides. Later, during the course of the evening after almost everyone had gone home, literally dozens of people called to see if they were needed to help during the shutdown. Some employees who had gone home hours earlier drove back many miles just to make sure everything was all right.

Later, when the power returned, the people who came in for the third shift capped off this remarkable display by doing an outstanding job in returning the plant to full operation.

Please accept my congratulations. I'm grateful to you for showing this kind of spirit toward your company and the people with whom you work.

Humor, when well done, works even in memos of praise.

I told Janet that I thought the July Newsletter was the best yet. Then I found out that *you* wrote it. Now Janet isn't talking to me.

Great job!

      Jim Lavenson
      President of The Plaza

To a sales representative who won a monthly contest, from the head of the production department.

Fantastic is the word for your continued—and consistent—batting average, putting you right out front in the league.

We are, indeed, proud of your achievements and will do all we can at our end to keep you clicking.

Right on, man!

From the head of a wire and cable company to a salesman who has landed a big one.

My personal congratulations on your outstanding sale. It always brings a thrill of satisfaction to see company teamwork in action.

We are grateful for your efforts and applaud them vigorously.

From an account executive to a copy chief who has just come up with a new and promising campaign. Here's one way to handle the star for whom praise is an old story.

When the master exhibits his mastery there's a tendency to accept it matter-of-factly: "Why, of course, he's doing great things. It's expected. . .."

But your admirers on the staff continue to be impressed. Thanks, and continue to brighten our future.

From the head of production to the purchasing agent, who was able to come up with a large amount of a much-needed raw material.

You've done it again! Another great maneuver on the scarce-supply front—proving your skills as a one-man army and earning the Medal of Honor from a grateful colleague.

Need I say more?

To a design engineer, from the company president. The heart of the message here is recognition of the efforts made.

Thanks to you, the Ames project is moving ahead successfully. We're all very much aware of the amount of effort—to say nothing of the creativity—that has gone into your part of the program. You have won our gratitude and admiration.

Both praise and monetary reward to a deserving middle-manager. This memo was sent by the personnel director, but it's a type of message that may be sent by the recipient's boss, or, to make it a matter of greater moment, the boss's boss. Of course, when praise is coupled with a material reward, that's saying it with music.

During the past year, our company forged ahead to new heights of increased sales and earnings. Such growth is even more notable for this particular period since our national economy softened considerably. Many companies caught in the spiral of increasing costs and diminishing sales gains literally lost their profitability.

We recognize your key role in our business success—both currently and for the future. In a review of your responsibility with Mr. Sam Blaine it was decided to increase your salary beginning January 1 to the annual rate of $20,500.

You should be proud of your personal attainment. We need your continued extra effort —especially during the forthcoming year—for, with the advent of still further expansion, ever-increasing costs, and even more competition in the field—only extraordinary commitment by each of us will keep us successful.

Happy New Year to you and your family!

PROGRESS REPORTS

You're performing a task assigned to you by your superior. It's one that has to be done over a period of time. It becomes mutually desirable for you to let him know where you stand at a given time and how matters are going.

The progress report is also a control tool, like a safety gauge on a steam line. It can alert someone to an impending crisis or reassure by the assertion that everything is going according to plan.

This is the text of a memorandum, first reported by Washington news columnist Jack Anderson, from Mrs. Dita D. Beard, ITT Washington lobbyist, to W. R. Merriam, chief of the ITT Washington office. The text was made available by Anderson, and is reprinted here with permission of the Congressional Quarterly, *in which it appeared March 11, 1972.*

PERSONAL AND CONFIDENTIAL

Date: June 25, 1971

To: W. R. Merriam
From: D. D. Beard
Subject:
San Diego Convention

I just had a long talk with EJG (E. J. Gerrity, ITT's public relations chief). I'm so sorry that we got that call from the White House. I thought you and I had agreed very thoroughly that under no circumstances would anyone in this office discuss with anyone our participation in the convention, including me. Other than permitting John Mitchell, (Calif. Lt. Gov.) Ed Reinecke, Bob Haldeman and Nixon (besides Wilson, of course) *no one* has known from whom the 400 thousand commitment had come. You can't imagine how many queries I've had from "friends" about this situation and I have in each and every case denied knowledge of any kind. It would be wise for all of us here to continue to do that, regardless of from whom any questions come, White House or whoever. John Mitchell has certainly kept it on the higher level only, we should be able to do the same.

I was afraid the discussion about the three hundred/four hundred thousand commitment would come up soon. If you remember, I suggested that we all stay out of that, other than the fact that I told you I had heard Hal (Harold Geneen, ITT president) up the original amount.

Now I understand from Ned that both he and you are upset about the decision to make it four hundred in *services*. Believe me, this is not what Hal said. Just after I talked with Ned, (Rep. Bob) Wilson called me, to report on his meeting with Hal. Hal at no time told Wilson that our donation would be in services ONLY. In fact, quite the contrary. There would be very little cash involved, but certainly some. I am convinced, because of several conversations with Louie (former Kentucky Gov. Nunn) re Mitchell, that our noble commitment has gone a long way toward our negotiations on the mergers eventually coming out as Hal wants them. Certainly the President has told Mitchell to see that things are worked out fairly. It is still only (antitrust chief Richard) McLauren's mickey mouse we are suffering.

We all know Hal and his big mouth! But this is the one time he cannot tell you and Ned one thing and Wilson (and me) another!

I hope, dear Bill, that all of this can be reconciled—between Hal and Wilson—if all of us in this office remain totally ignorant of any commitment ITT has made to anyone. If it gets too much publicity, you can believe our negotiations with Justice will wind up shot down. Mitchell is definitely helping us, but cannot let it be known. Please destroy this, huh?

A customer-service manager informs her superior on progress in dealing with a bottleneck.

Here it is the first of the month and we've processed half the backlog of customer requests. In other words, we're right on target, and so I expect that by the end of next week, we'll be caught up.

A promotion manager reports to his boss, vice-president of sales, on the production of a film strip which is to be used as the basis for a new sales presentation.

You ask about the status of the sales presentation film strip. I've just checked with the producer, and here's the story:

The script, first draft, should be in our hands within ten days. If corrections are minor, which is what I expect, add two or three days for revision.

We should allow about a month for art and photography. But during this same period we'll select an actor and record the narration.

With time for processing and a normal amount of slippage, we should have the first strip ready for viewing by the end of June. This schedule makes it possible for us to make the

184

presentation changeover starting in September.

I'll keep you informed as to how closely we're meeting this schedule.

Not on schedule, but a suggestion opens the way for a better showing.

At our present rate of output, we will miss the deadline on the Jackson order by about a week. Here's our performance to date:

Week ending 2/1—24 assemblies

"   "   2/8—19 assemblies

"   "   2/15—25 assemblies

Assuming that this week's production will be 25 units, we'll be 17 short of the 110 ordered. I estimate that if we authorize overtime, we could complete the job in three days less. Think it's worth doing?

A mail-order executive of a publications firm briefs the president on the status of an operation.

As my shaky boat sails slowly down (up?) the well-known creek, I thought I'd drop you a line in case anyone ever asks, "How the hell did *that* happen?"

The "that" which is about to happen is *nothing* and the date is *June 26* and the trouble is that we should be sending out a test mailing for the next publication on that day. Here's why we'll be forced to skip the mailing:

Ed Radey and I got together over the copy of the letter that the outside writer did for us and agreed that it just doesn't have it. Not only doesn't it represent the product in a sufficiently attractive way, but the feel for the audience—that we've spent months analyzing—isn't there.

Also unhelpful have been the editorial department's last-minute changes of heart and mind on the thrust of the product.

At the moment I am trying to play two horses. Rawson has promised me a first draft of his version of a letter by next Wednesday, June 14. While it would take a miracle for this to be so perfect that it could go to the printer on the 16th, there is the possibility that I might be able to process it to the point where Ed or some other volunteer could follow up on it. The second alternative is for me to wait, close my door, and see what kind of a miracle I can pull off on updating one of our old letters. If I am lucky, both of these pieces will pan out. If not, please address all future mail care of "creek."

PROMOTIONS

Promotions of employees (at all levels) are big events in the world of business. Certainly when a company acquires a new head, the entire organization is likely to be affected and should be notified.

But on a less grand scale it is still true that to the man who's being advanced the event has great significance. There are often strong feelings involved in even the most obscure promotion. A memo written in this subject area may want to take into account some of the feelings of pleasure, delight, satisfaction, etc.

But a promotion memo may have additional purposes or consequences; employees can be reminded that the organization does encourage upward mobility; a top executive can make it clear that he endorses the promotion, backs the promotee; colleagues can be informed of the nature of the new responsibility, limits of the job, title, etc.

The personnel department announces some promotions to all employees.

It is always a pleasure to recognize superior performance. Finance Vice-President Peter Lewis has asked us to announce the following promotions:

Terry Caputo from Accounting Manager to Controller.

Henrietta Malnik from Accounting Supervisor to Accounting Manager.

Joy Parcells from Divisional Financial Advisor to Manager, Financial Planning.

We would like to take this opportunity to congratulate them and wish them well in their new positions.

Vice-president of marketing announces two promotions to the sales forces. See the next two examples for related messages. Also, notice the "sell" quality of the memos. For example, the vice-president's announcement makes clear his enthusiasm and optimistic expectations and adds his personal endorsement.

I am delighted to announce a change, as of February 1, in our sales management structure which will improve our operations as well as recognize the talents of the two men involved.

Peter Groves will be Director of Marketing. Pete has been in charge of most of our marketing in the past, but the new job envisages his spending more time on planning, merchandising, and liaison with production and the business office.

Ben Sanders will be National Sales Manager and report directly to Peter Groves. The regional directors, service managers, and the field sales force will report to Ben.

You'll be hearing from Pete and Ben during the next few days. We are all fortunate to have these two men help us capitalize on a very exciting future.

Peter Groves, newly promoted director of marketing, has his say on the new setup. The memo below is a second follow-up.

For almost twenty years, I have been associated with some of you as a fellow salesman or regional supervisor, and for the past seven years, as your sales manager. I can assure you, I have enjoyed every minute of each activity.

Of course, my successor, Ben Sanders, is no stranger to any of you. In addition to his fine record in field sales and regional management, Ben is a great guy, a truly professional salesman, and an understanding leader. You'll now work directly with Ben Sanders but, having total responsibility, I'll be interested as always in your concerns, your progress, your personal success. I assure you that this coming year will reflect continuous growth and success for all.

Ben Sanders, newly appointed national sales manager, makes a statement on the new situation.

Notice that each of the three memos in the series clarifies who will be responsible for what. And the personal tone humanizes the entire procedure.

I have known and worked with many of you for over twenty years and with some of you for a much shorter period of time, but with no less satisfaction. In writing you as national sales manager for the first time, I must admit to a sense of excitement and anticipation!

There has never been a time that I was more

firmly convinced that our direction is right; that our products are consistently improving; and that we have a more capable group of trainees, district managers, and regional directors than right now.

Being able to work closer with each of you, therefore, gives me a feeling of elation and optimism in what I know we can collectively accomplish in the coming year.

Chairman of a paper company announces a promotion—actually a shift from one vice-presidency to another.

Lewis Coates has been named Executive Vice-President—Finance. In his new position, Mr. Coates will be the chief financial officer of the company and will have functional responsibility for all financial operations and resources. Mr Coates is also a member of the board of directors.

Prior to this appointment, Mr. Coates was Executive Vice-President—Administration. Before joining XYZ in that position, Mr. Coates had been vice-president in charge of the Finance Division of Northern Electric Company. His diversified career with that company spanned some twenty-five years and included both staff and line responsibilities in finance, personnel, purchasing, and manufacturing.

A former U.S. Navy officer, Mr. Coates served in naval intelligence and supply corps units during World War II. He holds B.S. and M.A. degrees in business administration and a Ph.D. degree in economics from Columbia University.

Mr. Coates is a member of the Telephone Pioneers of America and the American Economic Association. He is also a member of the advisory board of the Red Cross and United Fund of America.

Enter a new marketing director.

I am pleased to announce the appointment of Jane Smith as Marketing Director of Stone Products, Inc.

Ms. Smith's effectiveness in the sales area of this company has earned her this title.

PROPOSALS

(*see also* Ideas; Persuasion; *and* Suggestions)

There are occasions where nothing is ever accomplished without a proposal. An idea is described, evaluated, sometimes with objectivity, more often with a bit of sell that reflects the proposer's love. The proposal memo may be the starting gun of a chain of events leading to its implementation.

When a proposal is made and rejected there can be two reasons: it's a poor idea or it's been inadequately presented. Many a good proposal had gone down the drain because it looked or sounded unimpressive.

Unfortunately, good ideas have been killed by poor proposals and unworthy ones have been acted on because, perhaps, a proposal was more effective than it should have been.

The proposal memo is an important means by which an executive can make his ideas known and accepted. In some companies, a form is devised to simplify the procedure of making a proposal. A sample of one such form is included in this section (see the first item).

A supervisor submits a proposal to his boss for a change in the locker room setup. The form used is simple and may be applied to a variety of such messages.

DATE: JUNE 12, 197–.

SUBJECT: Plan to change locker room location.

PROBLEM: Present location is inconvenient.
Time lost by workers between work area and lockers totals about twelve minutes per day per worker. (Include additional points as required.)

PROPOSAL: Move lockers to B storage room; using present locker room for storage.

ADVANTAGES: Lockers would be next door to work area. (Include additional points as required.)

DISADVANTAGES: Change would occupy two men for three days. (Include additional points as required.)

RECOMMENDATIONS: Locker location should be changed because it will save time and will be a morale builder worth the expense involved.

Ed Loman
Supervisor

Selznick writes to a Metro-Goldwyn-Mayer vice-president about a cost-saving idea. But David Copperfield *was eventually released as one film.*

To: E. J. Mannix   April 24, 1934

. . . in discussion with Nick [Schenck] today told him that could make two pictures out of "David Copperfield" for probably hundred thousand dollars more than one picture and produce them so that each picture would be complete in itself. Possibly releasing second several months after first, or possibly releasing them together for exhibition during succeeding weeks. Nick surprised me be saying that plan was excellent one and we should by all means proceed with it. . . .

Memo From David O. Selznick

A member of the public relations staff sends a memo to one of her own company's executives.

Although we wanted this trade publication to do a personal interview with you, they claim it doesn't fit their style. However, by dint of acquiring the reputation as the best nudge of the year, I've extracted a tentative promise for a 700-word feature story, provided they approve a one-page outline. Knowing you don't like to write, how about working it out this way: Give me the bare bones of the kind of story you'd like to see in print. We'll develop the outline, and if approved, we'll arrange to write it under your byline.

A feature page in this publication would, I think, be very impressive. Hope you agree.

A promotion manager writes to a sales executive. Notice how the purpose of the

We made our Customer Service Guide available in July 1973. Nine months have passed since *proposal is clearly stated, both by words and structure.*

that date and it's desirable, I feel, for us to conduct a survey to find out what's been happening.

As you may remember, we produced this tool as a result of a widespread request from the field. It was felt that in many instances sales could be made that otherwise might not be to companies who were interested in our product line.

I'm in favor of a survey at this time, whose objective would be to assess:

• how well the guide has fared in view of our expectations;

• what we can do in the future to make the guide a more effective sales promotion tool.

Let me know your reaction to the above.

A bookstore manager asks his boss to give raises to two of his employees. This is an interesting example of the free-flowing style of the new (post-1970) type of manager. This is an interesting and fluent example of a manager going to bat for his employees.

There is a position in the bookstore that, upon quittance by the former occupant, was made a temporary one. I do not believe that was fair, since the position was never evaluated by anyone higher than yours truly. Nevermind! Lava under the bridge! My considered opinion just happens to be that the work *can* be absorbed by the two people left.

But, given that, it is my opinion that we have an adjustment to make. Tony Loy moved his family up here from Connecticut to take the job, which pays $5,200 per annum. Fred Grail has a new baby, food stamps and $5,200 per annum. If you think I am shaking the tambourine, you are right! They both have been here almost a year and have shown a large capacity for work, and a talent for what they are doing. What are you willing to show them?

I believe that two people who have most immediate needs, who have demonstrated their quality, and who are willing to take on additional tasks, should be compensated in some way. It's time to put your money where your mouth is!

A department head in an industrial products firm sends a suggestion to the

As sales figures continue to sag, I, along with others have sought ways for improvement. I *vice-president in charge of marketing. The basic nature of what's suggested—creating, in effect, a new job and new type of sub-organization in the company—clearly would require a great deal of follow-up discussion. That is, if it's considered at all.*

think it's likely that a number of product changes could increase product appeal—perhaps including a change of mix. I'm certain, however, that such changes in the present situation are palliatives.

One promising alternative in my opinion is the recruitment of a project manager, a man with fresh energies, a knowledge of our business, market oriented, who would report to top management, have responsibility for both sales and production, and would unite the strengths and mobilize the capabilities of both.

Agreed, the project manager must have unique qualities, not easily come by, and would probably be available at a minimum of $30,000. Such an investment is large and risky. But in view of the alternative, it would seem like a do-or-die decision. The same man could possibly take on other responsibilities, providing a little more budgetary leeway.

I realize that precedent is unfavorable. Previous attempts to bring in can-do men at the managerial level have notably failed. But I believe the size of the stakes warrants the gamble. In the face of falling sales volume, it can only be a matter of time before drastic action must be taken. Perhaps we're approaching that decision point. There are other aspects to this suggestion that could be discussed, but for now, I would like to get your reaction to the basic idea.

PROTESTS

(*see also* Complaints *and* Disagreement)

Actions may be taken, events may develop, which one finds unacceptable. There's a desire to protest against them, either to the people involved or to a higher authority. Where the writer has strong emotional involvements, he must take particular pains to make sure that the wording of his message will not suffer as a result. This caution does not mean watering down a message. It does mean making a statement in a rational framework and in a reasonable way to increase the validity of the objection.

It may be unwise to protest just for the sake of protesting, that is, for the record, since the writer's view may prove wrong. But in any event, the protest should be given a constructive angle so that some worthwhile counteraction may be suggested and undertaken.

A movie producer writes to his director about a work problem.

To: Mr. Richard Boleslawski   June 17, 1936

Dear Boley:

Would you *please* speak to Marlene about the fact that her hair is getting so much attention, and is being coiffed to such a degree that all reality is lost. Her hair is so well placed that at all times—when the wind is blowing, for instance—or when Marlene is on a balcony or walking through the streets—it remains perfectly smooth and unruffled; in fact, is so well placed that it could be nothing but a wig.

The extreme in ridiculousness is the scene in bed. No woman in the world has ever had her hair appear as Marlene's does in this scene, and the entire scene becomes practically unusable because everything is so exactly in place that the whole effect of a harassed and troubled woman is lost.

Even today, on the set, having the hairdresser rush in between takes to put each last strand of hair in place looked so nonsensical, when you could see the palms blowing in the background.

Surely a *little* reality can't do a great beauty any harm.

I wish you would go over the contents of this note with Marlene, who, I am sure, will realize that what I say makes sense; and if you will remind me, I will go into it with you and Marlene again when I am next on the set.

DOS

Memo From David'O. Selznick

The writer, whose name is spelled Burger, strikes back at the misspellers who substitute an e *for the* u.

Recent research turns up the following on the spelling of names:

"A rose by any other name would smell as sweet (even though it might be spelled differently)."—Gertrude Stein

"Some people are compulsive, some people are permissive, but everyone has strong feelings about the use of his name."—Psychological Abstracts, Vol. IV, page 5471

"If you don't know how to spell, go back into the schoolroom."—Harry Truman.

This is absolutely my next-to-the last word on the subject.

Signed,　u
Ruth Bérger
Ruth Burger
Research Institute of America

From an office manager to a shop fore-man, protesting the behavior of the latter's subordinates.

As you know, I'm a strong partisan of personal liberties and the live-and-let-live principle. But the conduct of some of your people out in the yard during rest periods has passed acceptable limits.

The first problem is the simple one of noise. As you know, our office windows look out on the yard, and the pickup ball games lead to so much shouting and yelling that it interferes with the work of my people.

The second point has to do with appearance. Some of your men, under the guise of sun bathing, are walking around in their undershorts. It's fine for the beach. It certainly looks like hell on company premises.

I hope you can do something about the situation before it has to be brought to the attention of others. I'd like to think we can settle this between ourselves.

One supervisor asks another to stop giving one of his employees "assignments."

Janice told me again today that you have been asking her to do copying for you "because she's near the machine" and "it'll only take a minute."

I consider these requests an imposition on Janice and an annoying intrusion on my area of responsibility. Please don't permit this situation to continue.

QUERIES

See Inquiry

REASSURANCE

A subordinate who has failed in a key project, or one who is unsure of his job, may have spirits raised by an appropriate message. Whenever people have doubts and uncertainties, upsets result which can be painful. If you're in a position where a relevant message will improve their situation, it's an act both of kindness and good management to send it.

A newly promoted executive tells an ex-subordinate that he'll still be at hand to render assistance if needed.

You were kind enough to send me a nice note in connection with my recent promotion. You also voiced some concern that the new state of affairs would leave you without the benefit of my "guidance." I believe you're exaggerating the degree to which I've been of help. You know I've always considered you to be a very talented and capable person.

However, be assured that the change in my

situation will not make me any less accessible. If in the future I can be of any help, you know my door is always open.

A higher echelon executive to a lower level manager who is concerned about his job.

Yes, I've been hearing some of the same rumors of reorganization and ruin that you have. I'm sure of two things:

They're exaggerated. While there may be some changes made, the company is quite healthy and will be around for a long time to come.

Your own situation is promising. You've made a good reputation for yourself, and the company will surely continue to require your services.

Obviously, I wouldn't put this in writing if I weren't pretty sure of my facts. So, chin up and don't waste your time worrying.

A field representative, badly shaken by home-office credit decisions made with respect to his customers, gets a reply to his question, "Where does it leave me?"

Thanks for your 7/30 answer to our note on the Farley and National billing situation.

Yes—we did cancel the credit memo to Farley and did issue a new one to National.

To answer your entreaty, "What can I ever do to clear up my reputation as the Angry Warrior with my customers . . . ?"

First—Gary, don't worry about *your* reputation. After putting in the many hard successful years that you have with the company you are universally held in high esteem.

Second, remember that we share the same company goals, aims, and targets. And, just as you encounter perplexing field conditions—we here come up against frustrating personnel and processing problems.

Working these matters out *together* for the benefit of the many concerned is what makes our team the very best in the business.

Please, Gary, keep throwing that proverbial ball to us; and, we promise we'll, in turn, do our very best in fielding it properly for you.

RECOMMENDATIONS   (*see also* Advocacy)

You wish to put in a good word for somebody, or espouse a cause, come out in favor of a course of action. Nine times out of ten such messages are innocuous. But the tenth occasion may mean you're sticking your neck out, particularly if what you're backing is controversial—for example, an unpopular employee. Generally, we're in favor of risk-taking—but it's your neck. Before writing this type of memo, ask yourself, "Will I be sorry I sent it if the person or thing I backed flops?"

In some situations, the initiative is out of your hands: your boss asks you to make recommendations about some matter. In this context, your espousal is a form of decision-making, and should be based on decision-making procedures, consideration of alternatives, evaluation of these, etc.

An executive, asking for his opinion, favors starting a house organ.

You asked for my views on starting a company newspaper. I recommend it, although I'm very much aware of the pros and cons of such an undertaking. There are all kinds of problems in simply producing the house organ on a regular basis, getting volunteers, appointing an editor, and the touchy problem of setting policy. Nevertheless, I believe there are some important needs such a medium would fill for us right now. A major one is top management's contact with employees. As a result of our being acquired several years ago, there is confusion in the collective mind of our employees about just what local management is, how we operate, and so on. I don't know how much of this fog we can eliminate, but I'm sure that we need more contact and communication than we've had. In short, I'm in favor of starting a company newspaper or magazine as soon as possible.

From the department head to the division manager, on the matter of new personnel. Note that instead of detailing the reasons for his views, he saves those for a face-to-face meeting. This is a good

Here are my recommendations regarding personnel for next year.

Based on the experience of the past nine months and my view of what the new schedules mean regarding workload, I recommend that we *way to avoid lengthy memos stating a case which is better developed by the other person's questions and responses.*

add one engineer in the $18,000–$20,000 range and one permanent three-day-a-week secretary.

The engineer is primarily a strengthening for our production improvement efforts. The secretary will be similar to the one we had the first half of this year, and will work primarily to assist the staff with reports, and general correspondence, as well as other clerical duties.

Rather than give lengthy explanations of the need for these people in this memo, I will be glad to support the recommendation in a meeting at your convenience.

A plant superintendent makes a recommendation to a production manager about replacing outworn equipment.

In walking through your department the other day I was struck by the dilapidated condition of the tote boxes used for assembly parts and finished work. I think there are three good reasons for replacing these now:

Safety. Increased convenience. Increased efficiency.

To achieve this third benefit I think you should come up with a new design so that we get the optimum size and shape for the work that you're processing now.

Recommendation for a separated employee. You'll find more memos for this situation under the next heading, References.

Gary Bohn has worked for me for the past three years and I've found him to be a capable and dependable machine operator. As you know, the only reason he's being let go is that the new automatic punch press means termination for all but our highest seniority press operators.

If you have a job for him you'll be acquiring a good man. I recommend him most strongly.

REFERENCES

References are statements, usually laudatory, made about subordinates who leave your employ. Usually they are meant to assist a person in getting another job. But there is a situation *within* an organization in which a "reference" is appropriate. This is the case when an employee is being transferred to another department. Or, if you are moving out of your position, you may leave a statement about a subordinate for your successor.

The intracompany reference is somewhat more personal than the standard variety, since it's a message going to another member of the organization family, rather than the traditional, "To whom it may concern." The aim in writing such a memo is to be helpful both to the employee and his new boss. It's possible that an antagonistic executive might want to even an old score with an unsatisfactory employee by writing an unfavorable note. Fortunately, such memos are rare, and are generally undesirable.

But executives have another practical reason to avoid derogatory statements. For example, a manager feels that a transferee is a sarcastic and abrasive individual. But he realizes that this quality was one that tended to develop out of his particular relationship with the employee. With another boss the employee's behavior might change considerably. No matter how hostile one feels, because of past dealings, it's wise to give the employee the benefit of the doubt and the chance to develop in his new job without the handicaps of past failures.

This simple note confirms the transfer, makes a helpful point about working with the employee, and is appropriately optimistic about the outcome.

As we agreed, next week Pete Farson is being transferred to your department. I think you will find that Pete is quick on the uptake and that he will perform particularly well when he is clear on job objectives and given a free rein. I am sure there will be mutual benefits for you and Pete Farson in this new association.

Blanket praise launches the transferred employee into the new situation with all flags flying. The comment about unused potential is made in a constructive way and could be helpful to both Jane and her new boss.

Jane Goodwill worked as my secretary for six years. In that time I had every reason to feel lucky to have her as an assistant. She is bright, quick, and has excellent judgment.

There is one personal note I would like to add: In the last year that Jane worked for me I became aware that I had never delegated some jobs that were well within her capability. Unfortunately, our working patterns and relationship had been pretty well established and I found it difficult to make the change, no matter how desirable it might have been.

Perhaps you can benefit from this personal shortcoming of mine. I have the feeling that it would help Jane enjoy her work even more and make it possible for her to operate at a level closer to her real potential.

The writer has something on his mind —obviously reflecting some unsatisfactory experience he has had with the employee. But the memo is carefully worded, and well balanced. Note that Claude comes in for specific praise, to offset the implied criticism for his tendency to want to run the show.

Mr. Cahill has finally persuaded me to let Claude Courbet transfer to your department. Despite my original hesitation to go along with the idea—basically, I think it's a bad precedent to encourage employees to shop around looking for better jobs from one department to the next—I am now perfectly agreeable. And it's not because I am glad to get rid of Claude. On the contrary. He made many notable contributions in my unit. He is particularly good in thinking up fresh solutions to old problems—which is a rare skill indeed.

The one suggestion I do make—and I make it tentatively—is that at least at the beginning you keep him on a short leash. He has a tendency to want to take over the work completely on his own. This is a virtue—up to a point. But beyond that, it can lead to undirected or misdirected effort that can represent expensive wastes of time.

Naturally, I hope the transfer works out for Claude and you.

REFUSAL

A turndown may be your best response to a request—that you attend a meeting, be a featured speaker, and so on. Since the nature of the message almost automatically creates disappointment, you may want to take special pains to soften the blow.

A manager begs off attending a meeting and offers a reasonable, though standard, excuse.

Much as I'd like to, I'll have to turn down the invitation to attend your meeting next week. Unfortunately, it conflicts with something I already have scheduled.

A vice-president writes to a committee chairman, with a touch of humor to coat the pill.

You'll be happy to know that I'm refusing your request to speak at the company dinner next month. The reason is, quite frankly, I don't do too well on the speaker's platform.

However, since I'm eager to contribute to the success of your affair, perhaps there are some other duties I can perform. Please don't hesitate to ask.

Firm, but with an explanation.

No, No, a thousand-and-one times No! Please do not store any packing cases in operating areas of my department. I know you say "it will only be for a short while," but we both know how temporary storage tends to become permanent. Second of all, such storage would be a safety hazard.

This is my final word. If you should want to go higher up with your request, I'd still fight it. But I'm hoping you have some practical alternative that will solve your problem.

This refusal is based on pointing to an error.

Sorry, Eileen, but I can't accept the copying charges for that marketing report. True enough, the material originated in my department. But after all, the copies are going to be sent elsewhere. If anything, I think this is a Market Research item. See what you can do.

REGRETS (*see also* Condolences)

An event has taken place that is deplorable or unfortunate. It can be anything from an appointment missed to a development that had created a real hardship for an individual. It's important in this type of message to avoid having wordiness drown out the sincerity of the message. See how the models under this heading accomplish this purpose.

Postponement because of a matter of higher priority.

Can't tell you how sorry I am that our get-together this morning didn't come off. As my secretary explained, I got an unexpected call from the front office which I couldn't defer. I hope you weren't too badly inconvenienced. Can we reschedule our meeting?

An executive tells a colleague he'll be unable to accept an invitation to a daughter's nuptials.

Both Helen and I very much appreciate the invitation to your daughter's wedding. As you know, we've seen her grow up. I still remember her first visit to the office here, a lively bouncing young lady of ten or twelve.

But, as you know, Helen hasn't been feeling well, and it's quite impossible for her to make the trip. Please let me have your daughter's home address because we'd like to wish her the best and celebrate the event in some tangible way.

"It won't happen again."

Awfully sorry you had that mess in your office when the hand truck one of my men was pushing cracked your water cooler. I hope the cleanup squad that I rushed over was able to minimize the damage.

Of course we can't undo the mess, but I have instructed my people to use another route in getting around the building with hand trucks.

REMINDERS

If people had built-in alarm clocks or tickler files this type of memo would never have to be written. But unfortunately under the pressure of getting out the work, etc., we sometimes forget agreed-upon appointments or obligations. A reminder memo can make sure that the proper people remember to go to a meeting or to have some action started or consummated, and the memo can be timed so as to make any necessary preparation possible.

A construction company president to his management people about a dinner

Last call! Last week to get in your reservation for the company's quarterly management din-

202

that's been planned. The "sell" is meant to build up the turnout.

ner! Let Martin Moore know your intentions as soon as possible. Don't miss out on an evening guaranteed to provide good food, good drink, and good fellowship. Special surprise entertainment. Come! You'll be so glad you did.

A division head writes to his supervisors. No harm in the sugar-coating close.

This is just an early warning signal that your budget estimates are due in my office by Friday, November 16. The reason for the deadline is that the company's overall figures have to be in the treasurer's office by November 23.

Work now, play later.

Selznick writes to the company attorney about salary and related matters.

March 26, 1930

Dear Henry [Herzbrun]:

All kidding aside, I hope you remember our talk at the time my contract was signed about my salary on my wedding trip; and I hope also that Ben [Schulberg] remembers he promised Irene and myself we could have this. As to the number of weeks please remember that while I was entitled to two weeks vacation each year, I have never taken it; and as I am in my third year here, the firm owes me six weeks on this alone. Also, I was supposed to get a vacation trip when Ben came back, but as you know, this deteriorated into a series of jobs in New York. So, all in all, I honestly think I am entitled to a couple of months. Also, I am sure the firm would like to see me get off to the right start. Think of all the extra work they are going to get out of me by my being a married man!

Memo From David O. Selznick

An executive nudges a colleague whose borrowing has passed a reasonable time limit—an occurrence as common as apples.

I see by my records that four weeks have passed since you borrowed my tape recorder. You said you wanted it just for a trial, so I imagine you've had enough time for this purpose. Since both I and my secretary use it fairly often, it's been somewhat of an inconvenience. Get on the ball, Ray! If you want one, buy one, but in any event, get mine back to me.

An editor in chief of a group of publications sends a memo to the editorial staff.

Please, when you pick up a story from another publication, always check the story for factual content with the editor of the other publication before it gets into print. And please, if you are the editor of that other publication, alert your fellow editors as soon as you become aware of any factual inaccuracy in a story you have printed.

Just this morning, for example, we were able to correct an embarrassing error because I remembered that a story that was going to press had an error in an earlier version. But we can't depend on chance. The only way we can minimize mistakes is for everybody to take responsibility for double checking. Like the man said, "It's better to be safe than sorry."

Occasionally, an executive makes a promise in public he regrets in private. Here an employee writes a company vice-president who had made optimistic assertions—he "promised" certain objectives would be met—and reminds him of his statement, also tactfully giving him a chance to get off the hook.

It's past the thirty-day limit you set for the developments that were supposed to answer my questions about market analysis and sales manpower. So far there's been nothing visible that approaches what you described.

Of course, we both know no explanation is necessary. But I was pleased at your recognition of my concern and thought you might like to have a second go at it.

A personnel director writes to department heads.

A reminder: the merit review forms are due back March 29. If there's any reason for delay, may I be of help?

A reminder in advance of a deadline can save an executive disappointment, or the need to bawl out a forgetful subordinate. Obviously, some subjects require stronger reminders than others.

Hope you haven't forgotten—deadline for your storage-area cleanup is the end of the week.

When repeated reminders fail, you're justified in getting a bit rough.

This is the third time I've had to ask you to return my copy of the company handbook. Several times I've been inconvenienced by not having it. Please don't make it necessary for me to write you about this matter again.

REMINDERS TO ONESELF

There are occasions when you are yourself the recipient of your own message. Usually this is a reminder to take some follow-up action, or to recall some situation, a verbal string around the finger. The implements of such self-communication are the deskpad or calendar, the tickler file, a pocket memo book, a note pasted on the wall or pinned on your personal bulletin board.

An executive makes an entry in his pocket memo book about his secretary's anniversary.	Wednesday, June 8, is Carrie's anniversary with the company. Make a reservation at Clint's for lunch and ask Personnel to send her a bunch of yellow roses.
A manager makes a note on his desk calendar about a deadline.	If Andy Cullen hasn't called me about the Davis shipment by this date, contact Davis directly.
Note taped to a manager's desk blotter.	Remind Bob that he's due for a merit review some time this week. Already two weeks overdue.
A manager jots down a message Friday afternoon on next Monday's page of his desk calendar.	Remember to look up the production rates of the M-16, to be able to give Sales a delivery date for the order for 1,000 pieces they asked about.
A woman executive clips a note to her handbag at home, to be implemented when she gets to the office.	Call Personnel first thing to ask for action on the summer replacement schedule.

REPLIES AND REJOINDERS

Since this type of memo is sometimes seen as an opportunity to exercise wit, the literature has been enriched by the wisecracking reply. Especially valued in the executive suite is the one word, or brief response that presumably "says it all." But aside from the opportunity for humor, this category is essential for the full exchange of information within a company. A particular aspect of this form is its timing. The common complaint, "I sent you a memo two weeks ago and still haven't got an answer," suggests a serious rupture of communication. If delay is unavoidable, it's better to write, saying that you don't have the needed information, you're trying to get it, or in some other way making it unnecessary for the questioner to be disappointed.

A story—possibly apocryphal—describes an effective nonverbal reply. Into the office of Robert Moses, the project planner responsible for the great Long Island oceanside development Jones Beach, came a memo from a field superintendent. The man was both puzzled and irate: there was an old barn on beach property he had to clear, and despite many inquiries, he had received no word on what to do with the structure. Would Mr. Moses please help solve the problem? Mr. Moses did. He sent the memo back to the sender with a wooden match taped to it.

Employees of a New York publisher were taken to task over what was considered overinformal dress, including "bare feet, bare midriffs, T-shirts, and so on." This is how the aggrieved staff responded.

Pillbox hats, veils, white gloves, stockings with seams, closed front and back shoes, matching shoes and handbags, skirts at the middle of the knee, Pan-Cake makeup, bras, girdles, Merry Widows, trusses, vaginal sprays, Evening in Paris perfume—while they were perfectly acceptable modes of attire in 1940 and for elderly spinsters, they are totally UNacceptable for employees of the publishers of some far-out fiction. After work you may look as dowdy as you like, but PLEASE not during the working day. Please bear in mind at all times that you do not work for the Girl Scouts of America.

Gerald Walker, an editor of The New York Times Magazine, did a clever review of a book in the form of an exchange of interoffice memos. The first memo registered mock embarrassment over a review from an outside writer who had completely misunderstood the book on which

Paul: Kill and pay, and send it out again to someone with a sense of humor. And take that idiot's name off our list.—Dave *he was commenting. The writer of the memo explains the error of "the clod we assigned to review the book" and asks his boss what to do about it. The memo at the bottom of page 205 is the answer.*

The president of a hotel writes in response to a member of the company's board of directors who pointed out that the hotel's prices were very high.

Charlie, I agree with you completely. There are two ways we can cut: our prices and your dividends.

> Jim Lavenson
> President of The Plaza

In response to a complaint from an employee that his office was too cold and the air-conditioning couldn't be turned down, the company president sent a new cardigan sweater from Bergdorf Goodman and a note.

Wear this until we can get the damn thing fixed. Hopefully this will be accomplished while this sweater is still in style.

> Jim Lavenson
> President of The Plaza

A project manager responds to a complaint from a salesman in the field. Of particular interest is the opening phrase explaining a delayed answer. Flu or not, true or not, the sting of an apparently ignored message or one for which an answer is belated, is made more acceptable by a white lie of this kind.

Just got back to work after a two-week battle with the flu, and found your comments about the Acme situation.

I am sending your memo on to Hank Burrus, because I am sure that over the course of the years we have developed an effective reply to customer complaints of this type. My remarks are made simply from my point of view as a project manager. Also, I don't want you to think that I believe our products are perfect. I will certainly circulate the copies of your memo to my staff and urge them to consider your comments very seriously.

Thanks very much for writing to me, and I hope we can give you some help.

In answer to an unrealistic proposal.

The dollars say no.

A rejoinder to an incomplete reply.

Please reread my original memo. Your answer doesn't cover two major points. I'll clarify, if necessary.

REPORTS, GENERAL

Of all types of interoffice communication, this is the category which can run longest —sometimes to hundreds of pages. There would be no benefit in including as a sample a report of great length. The matter of organizing lengthy material can just as well be demonstrated in shorter pieces, such as those you'll find in the pages ahead.

Those planning to use this form for coverage at length will find it useful to review Section 9, *Writing the Long Report.* The recommendations can help solve problems of organization and so on.

A personnel manager reports the result of a study to a recruiting executive—subject, the changing makeup of a group of supervisors.

. . . note the helpful use of eyecatchers (called bullets) to set off a sequence of paragraphs.

Attached is the tabulation of supervisory profile sheets as of December. A number of interesting points:

• The percent of supervisors in the 25–34 age bracket jumped from 31% to 43% in three years.

• The percent of supervisors who have completed college increased from 23% to 44%. The percent of supervisors with some college experience has climbed from 58% to 69%.

• Number of years in supervision has decreased slightly overall, with notable rise in Under-3-year group, from 22% to 30%.

It would appear that our supervisory group, like the population at large, is younger and better educated than ever before. However, before adopting this as a hard and fast conclusion, it will be interesting to compare these results with our survey of the operating managers' group. The results of that survey should be available in about three weeks.

. . . lists of figures usually speak louder than words.

Tabulation

Under 25	1%
25–34	43%
35–44	29%
45–54	21%
55–over	6%

Education:

Graduated elementary school	1%
HS, didn't graduate	6%

208

HS, graduated	79%
College, didn't graduate	25%
College, graduated	
(4% have masters or are	
working toward)	44%
Other	7%

Number of years as supervisor:

Under 3 years	30%
3–10 years	35%
11–20	22%
Over 20	12%
No answer	1%

. . . a brief wrap-up suggests what's going to happen next.

These figures have implications for hiring, training, and promotions in the supervisory group. We should discuss these—at a time of your convenience.

A bank officer describes a Grid Seminar he attended—so that the stay-at-homes may share his experience.

Opening paragraph might have provided all relevant information—place, sponsoring organization, name of session, etc.

Second paragraph gets right down to the description, which is nicely streamlined.

On Tuesday, July 20, I attended a half-day orientation session given by Doctors Robert Blake and Jane Mouton.

This was my first "live" exposure to the managerial grid, and even at this late date the concept holds up well. The audience was small (fifty people) but alert and interested. In the presentation, Bob Blake does the talking and Jane Mouton sits on the sidelines offering occasional suggestions and corrections. (She's pretty and sharp, he's pleasant—slightly bumbling, and unpretentious—all virtues, I thought.)

I was impressed by Blake's talk and matter-of-fact presentation—no flashy opening, no artificial humor. The lack of pomposity lends weight to what he has to say.

He started with the standard managerial grid, relating types of management leadership to the five key grid positions. (I won't bore you with these.) The second half of the three-hour session was devoted to Organizational Development. He says there are six phases to an effective program:

Listing and numbering points of a key aspect of the program is helpful.

1. Managers in the subject company learn the grid on a voluntary basis.
2. Pilot program starts Sub-units of the organ-

ization start analyzing themselves, their inter-departmental relations, conflicts, and so on.

3. The units then establish contact with one another and begin comparing findings.

4. The organization then begins to design an ideal abstract model of itself. In this phase of the program, Blake recommends the reading of Sloan's *My Years with General Motors*. In this book, Sloan develops basic points for designing a big business organization:

Key financial objectives
Nature of the business
Nature of markets
Organization structure
Policies
Development

Having done this for GM (as derived from Sloan's book) executives then discuss their own company covering same points.

5. Going from ideal model to rehabilitating present organization, divide it into sub-units and test each against the ideal. A key question: "If you don't have present people, equipment, traditions and procedures, how could you meet financial objectives?" And so on, through list of points.

6. Period of consolidation. Testing out, adjusting for slippage.

I thought the time and money for attendance well spent, and would recommend a Blake-Mouton seminar for any professional manager.

Here are some stimulating phrases that came up:

• Optimizing vs. idealizing.
• How do you handle conflict with *a.* subordinates; *b.* boss; *c.* colleagues?
• Who's the best kind of person to use as a "seed" in an organization to spread new ideas? (Blake says the worst "seeds" are crown princes, the best are tough-minded production people.)
• Antiorganizational creativity. People want to bugger the system.

The Blake-Mouton team have found the grid approach stretchable. A book will be coming out shortly applying it to marriage. They say they

Key lists—good.

Good wrap-up, good reporting.

From a member of the training staff of a large company, to the head of the training department.

This is a reasonably short and colorful coverage of a communications seminar.

are now working on a parent-teenage book using the same concept.

A final sidelight. I asked Blake whether, since the grid attempts to describe behavior (which can be complex motivationally), he didn't find some deficiencies or inadequacies. He said no.

A most interesting conference took place last week at the Belmont Plaza, run by the New York State School of Industrial and Labor Relations, associated with Cornell University. I was surprised at the attendance—close to 200 people from all over the country. Title of the program —"The Hidden Revolution in Management: The Use of the Cassette in Communication and Training."

One highlight, presented by a featured speaker was a presentation called "The Psychology of Cassette Creation." I'll describe it briefly. He played the identical short audio cassette three times. The sound was that of a small boy singing "America." The first time the cassette was heard alone. The second playing was accompanied by roughly twenty slides. They showed the boy, the Virginia countryside, lovely rivers, trees, etc. With the little boy's voice the effect was quite moving. The third playing was accompanied by twenty more slides. Similar scenery but the river had an old tire and beer cans in it, the country road was heavily littered, another slide was "PRIVATE—KEEP OUT" and the final slide simply said "EXIT." The audience was interested to see that the identical sound could be made to create such different reactions. What interested me most was that the sound, although identical in each case, was nevertheless essential to the impact every time.

Let me list a few of the attending companies to give you a picture of who was interested in spending $85, plus travel and hotel, for the conference:

Chase Manhattan Bank	Xerox Corp.
	Coca-Cola USA

Equitable Life
McGraw-Hill
Bristol-Myers Co.,
   Intl.
New Jersey Bell Telephone
Sun Oil Company
Mobil Oil Corp.
Travlers Insurance
   Co.

CIBA
Kentucky Fried
   Chicken
New York Stock Exchange
Eastman Kodak
Smith, Kline & French
   Labs
Eastern Airlines
J. C. Penney Co.

It's not a coincidence that this and the previous report both describe seminars attended by the writer. This is a common form of the longer memo, and suggests that reportorial skills can be an executive asset in such writing. Perhaps management would do well to have the better reporters be the ones to attend meetings of this type that are of interest to a group of company people.

In a few days I will be sending you a report on the SONY Video Cassette Conference plus their program catalog and a couple of other pieces of printed material. Having attended the two conferences recently, my reaction is that audio cassettes are far from dead, and in fact never will be, any more than print. Video and audio each possess powerful features, but because of the great difference in cost there will always be jobs that audio can do effectively.

REQUESTS   (*see also* Appeals)

Memos in this area go in all directions through the organization. One may ask for assistance, cooperation, and so on. This type of memo sometimes runs into trouble when it hovers on the edge of being overly demanding or truculent. We can learn from the spoken word here: a request with a smile is apt to get readier compliance than one made with a frown. In some cases, the request is a form of directive or order.

A production head asks his supervisors for information about safety expenditures. Spelling out precisely what's wanted is always desirable in a request memo.

I'd appreciate it if you would give me an estimate of the types, quantity, and approximate cost of safety equipment (not including machine guards, etc.) you expect to use during next year. We can then see how it matches up to the budget allotment for each department. Check with me if you have trouble identifying items that belong on this list.

A promotion manager writes to field salesmen.

Are you using a trade magazine in your territory? If so, won't you please drop me a note and let me know the name and address of the publication, so that I can send along copies of our trade press releases? The interest stimulated by this kind of editorial mention will pay off in presold customers and increased sales for you.

I can assure you that we are eager to obtain the greatest amount of publicity for you that we can.

"Please return those tools."

Will all those who have borrowed hand tools from the Maintenance Department please return them? We're actually being handicapped by a shortage. Please don't let this inconvenience be the penalty for our generosity.

An effort to form a carpool.

Carpooling, anyone? In view of the gas shortage, we're trying to share gas and expenses. Anyone interested in joining a car pool, send in his name, address, and transportation times to Personnel. We'll get back to you with possible arrangements.

From a sales manager (actually, from his secretary) to company service personnel. The request is made in a clearly specified form, to maximize clarity and make it easier for the details of the request to be followed.

Tuesday, February 5
Please make the following arrangements:
1. Have a sign addressed to the staff, that the recreation room will be closed all day Wednesday, February 6, put on doors of rec room.
2. Maintenance men should see Andy Ander-

son in the afternoon about arranging chairs in conference room, and tables for lunch in rec room for conferees. Conference room to be cleaned.

3. John Frazer to put twenty-five cans of assorted soda in rec room refrigerator. He is also to provide empty cartons for garbage disposal.

4. Maintenance men to put small coffee urn on table outside the conference room in the hall to provide staff with coffee.

Wednesday, February 6

At 8:15 A.M. Val Conti to make coffee available to conferees for breaks and luncheon.

Ashtrays, plastic drinking glasses, and pitchers filled with iced water to be placed on conference table. (Val will be provided with a copy of the agenda, for possible help in setting up lunch —buffet-style.)

At the end of the day, conference room is to be cleaned, ashtrays cleaned, glasses disposed of, and garbage emptied into containers provided for this purpose.

If you have any questions, please call Andy Anderson on Ext. 344.

Many thanks for your kind cooperation.

The editor of a house organ asks his volunteer staff to please, please submit copy. Should work. But a follow-up phone call to individuals will help.

It is my sad duty to report that we are in a critical situation on *Review* copy. Here we are due to go to press in five days, and the cupboard is embarrassingly bare. Please dredge your copy drawer and your conscience, and send along your contributions. If the only roadblock is lack of a subject, check with me. I've got a lot of stuff on backlog.

I promise you that all contributions will be gratefully accepted—if not necessarily tenderly dealt with. Thank you, good people.

RESIGNATIONS   (*see also* Dismissal)

The messages under this heading have a single point. It has to do with an individual leaving the organization. In most cases the memo of resignation is written by the person who is planning to go. A memo on the subject of resignation *might* be written by a superior requesting the departure of a subordinate. But such requests are seldom put down on paper. When they are they're confined to a single sentence: "I'd like to have your resignation on my desk by . . ."

Note that in the samples included, the tone may range from regret to cold matter-of-factness that sometimes hides irritation, anger, etc. One moderating idea: Since the resignee may be looking for another job, he may not want to burn bridges by saying anything too vitriolic.

Also, resignations in the form of announcements are written by a supervisor regarding one of his subordinates. You'll find samples of this type of message included among the models.

A superior explains the departure of one of the company's designers. It may be that another purpose of this memo is to let it be known generally that the place-mat production is to be curtailed. One would assume, however, that those involved would have been told earlier.

I regret very much to have to announce the resignation of Dora Tolliner. Dora's resignation flows from the fact that we have decided to temporarily discontinue production of additional items in the place-mat line.

Dora has agreed to stay on for a period of seven or eight weeks in order to complete work already started. We shall miss her sorely and wish her everything good for the future!

A resignation from a new-era executive reflects a rather personal note. Refreshingly direct and expressive.

To YOU and all of them:
I am leaving.
I am tired of apathy and alienation.
I am bored and lonely.
I am tired of idealists. They are impersonal and can kill me.
I have not been laid in a year and a half. Now, that's RESIGNATION!

An editor in chief reports on the departure of a staff writer.

I'm sorry to tell you that Larry Gordon is leaving us. As you may know, Larry became a two-day a week employee more than a year ago, so that he could pursue freelance writing. Now, his personal business is booming. While he will **no** longer be coming in on a regular basis, he assures me that we will see him often, since he will continue to contribute to some of our publications. At other times, you'll be able to find him typing madly in the wilds of Rockland County, and listening with amused detachment to radio news of commuter train delays.

Since Gridley is an executive with many years of service, you wouldn't be wrong to guess that some serious difficulties or differences led to this outcome. Since such terseness is an affront in itself, it's usually desirable to avoid this type of note in favor of something more gracious—no matter what the circumstances.

By mutual agreement, Philip Gridley's employment by this company has been terminated as of Friday, June 4.

A long-time employee, an assistant office manager, announces his resignation. See the item below for the company follow-up. To some, this may seem overly sentimental and personal, but if it reflects the feelings of the writer, it's just fine.

Today is my last day at Clemens.

After eighteen years, the decision to leave was the most difficult one I have ever had to make. I have made many warm and lasting friendships, and it is because of such friendships that my decision to leave was so difficult. One could not work for the company for so many years, and not feel that it has become a part of one's very existence.

Over the years I have grown in wisdom and stature because of the many fine associates that I have worked with, and I trust that some of my talents have contributed to our success.

To all of my friends, I would have preferred to say my farewells on a more personal basis, but being a sentimental fool, I chose the easy way out, with this note. I am sure that many of our paths will cross in the future, so in a sense this is not good-bye.

I wish each and every one of you all the success and happiness that the ensuing years can possibly bring.

The president of Clemens sends his announcement of the assistant office manager's leaving to the staff. This message is for the purpose of publicly expressing the company's feeling about the resignation.

You all have received Bart Woodley's letter of resignation.

It's always difficult when people who have worked together for any length of time take different paths. Bart has been with Clemens for many years and his friends will certainly miss him. All of us wish him the best in his new connection.

Good luck in the years ahead, Bart.

A senior editor announces the resignation of a member of his staff. Here the announcement of departure is coupled with an explanation of how the vacated responsibility will be handled.

I regret to have to tell you that Joe Scotti, who has been our acquisition editor in the trade department, will be leaving us January 31. All of us know what contributions Joe has made over the past three years, and we will miss him sorely, as much as we wish him the best luck in his new job.

For the time being, I will assume his responsibilities, and with the help of our competent staff, we will assure the continuity of our acquisition program.

A member of the home office sales staff leaves for greater opportunity.

This is to inform all of you with whom I have enjoyed working over the past ten years that on February 12 I will be leaving to join Rawlins, Inc., as Eastern Sales Manager.

As you can well imagine this was no easy decision to make considering all that I have learned here, the wonderful friendships I enjoy and the fun and excitement I have had.

Another factor which made my decision more difficult is the progress that has been made in making our programs the finest array of services available to businessmen anywhere. However, the opportunity at Rawlins is one which I cannot afford to overlook.

I hope that this will be an outstanding year for you and the company, and it is my determined wish that our friendship will continue for many years to come.

RESOLVES AND RESOLUTIONS

An executive may want to put down on paper a decision he has made about a future course of action. Sometimes it may be for his own benefit. Usually, however, the memo is intended to put the recipient on notice about the nature of the resolve.

One word of caution: Remember the inevitable fate of New Year's resolutions—which are said to be made to be broken. A message of this type should be reviewed in the light of possible changes of heart or mind.

A production engineer tells his boss how he feels about a current assignment.

Just want you to know that I'm going to stick with the chipping problem till hell freezes over, or the equivalent. In the end, we may have to go to a more expensive sheet. But that's a last resort. Meanwhile, I'm not going to fail for lack of trying.

The staff man responsible for recruiting puts himself on record with his boss, the sales manager. Obviously, the statement will have a strong motivating effect on the writer himself.

Some people keep their resolution-making for the new year. I make mine every time I'm dissatisfied with something—at the moment, the rate at which we're putting men in the field.

I'd like to put myself on record: it is my intention to add ten more salesmen to our roster by the end of August. I give you permission to utter catcalls and throw ripe tomatoes every time I pass you in the hall if I fail.

Man and computer will fail or succeed together.

I'll get the computer printout in your hands by the end of the week, or I'll make old Compie pop its gaskets.

A foreman registers a resolve but also lets his boss know there's a problem that may call for intercession.

Just want you to know, Boss, I'm not taking any more crap from Engineering. If they won't cooperate—the job just won't get done. And you'll know who's at fault.

SELF-PROTECTION

This type of message is strictly political. It's sent with the intention of creating a record of the sender's situation, point of view, or feelings at a given point in time. The idea is that in the light of subsequent developments the memo as written will protect him against misunderstandings or blame.

If the question of time charges comes up later, this production manager has an out.

I'm going along with Paul's request for another week of trials on the new grinder, but frankly, I think it's a waste of time. Don't you think we ought to charge our time to Paul's department?

This supervisor is telling his boss that he, the boss, has a problem.

Just want you to know that, as you suggested, I've told May Rollins that she can report back to work next Monday. I hope you're right about her, and that her performance will improve. I'll keep you informed.

Putting down the facts for the record, and a suggestion for a possible next step.

Although I feel company policy is wrong on the matter of Dave Zara's vacation, I'm sticking by the ruling that Personnel made. I don't think Dave is going to be satisfied, and if so, I'd like you to be in on the reconsideration of his request.

If a problem arises, he can now show he raised the question.

As I understand it, the policing of the West building is Hogarth's responsibility. If I'm wrong about this, in any way, please straighten me out.

"SELLING"

This is a special form of the proposal memo. The unique quality is the effort made to get acceptance. Occasionally you want to "sell" an activity, an accomplishment, to your boss, a colleague, etc. The purpose is to present whatever it is you're selling in a particularly favorable light, to make its benefits irresistible. The "selling" memo gets its approaches from the field of salesmanship, a highly refined and professional area. The samples in this section convey some of the ways in which this form can be made effective.

From a company president to his executive staff.

I'm fifty-three years old and fat.

In addition, I'm in lousy shape physically.

And I don't ever seem to get time to do anything about it. . . .

Well, all that's about to change. A new health spa is opening just a block away from our offices, at 963 Main Street. (See attached brochure.)

If it looks as though I'm shilling for the spa people—call it enlightened collaboration. We don't have room for recreation facilities, and I for one have felt the need for some exercise, and an etcetera pretty well summed up by sauna, steam baths, massage, and so on.

We've been able to get a group rate from the spa management—$300 a year per person.

If you're interested—see you at the exercycles!

A department head sells the idea of a working Saturday.

Want a fun assignment working with a great crew, and the chance to pick up a handful of sweet bucks? Of course you do! Then volunteer to work next Saturday on inventory. See Sam Todd if you're interested.

An executive sets out to sell a subordinate on accepting a new assignment. Note how the benefits of the move are stressed.

In making up your mind about the move to Boston—

Remember that it means a new responsibility for you and the chance to fill in some gaps in your experience.

You'll be working with Ed Albright, a great

guy and one from whom there's a lot be to learned.

The increase in salary is not inconsiderable.

You'll have all the time you need to be selective in finding living quarters.

The company will pay all expenses for the change, including the time needed for your wife to take care of things like school for the kids.

My family and I lived in Boston for five of the pleasantest years of our lives.

It's obvious that we're all hoping you'll decide favorably because we feel it will do both you and the company a lot of good.

Don't let me oversell you. . . . (That's supposed to be funny, Charles.)

From a sales promotion manager to a group of children's-wear sales representatives telling them of company promotion plans. The sample is included because it illustrates professional, wellpaced writing, alive with action words, phrases, etc.

To speed you on your way to new increased healthy profits in the La Pouffette, Sweet Sixteen, and Imagination coordinated groups launched for Spring buying, we have prepared a trade advertising program that will help you tell your story!

The news explodes on January 3 in a two-page full-color insert in the Spring Buying edition of *Women's Wear,* the bible of the industry. The insert will be on a shining black background with the multi-print colors featured on one side of the page and several of the La Pouffette styles on the other side, all done in wide-awake color. The same two-page insert will be featured in *McCall's Children's Wear Merchandiser.* As you can see, this news will burst upon the entire industry and we predict that you will have as many people calling on you for information as you will be going out to call upon yourself.

Wait, there's more! *Earnshaws*—Infant's and Children's magazine has promised us substantial editorial coverage of the new coordinated sets. When will these editorials be run? In January, of course! *Corset and Brassiere Magazine* and *Corset and Underwear Review,* two of the most widely read publications in the brassiere field, have also promised January editorials.

There will be several others, but we will let you know somewhat later on, as we receive definite information about the exact timing of the editorials. Just be certain that we are constantly alert to obtain the kind of publicity for you that will add up to sales and to create the kind of advertising that will say to your customers that TEENFORM means elegance.

Did you think we were finished? Not at all! On February 6 Celanese Corp. will cooperate with TEENFORM on an ad in *The New York Times Sunday Magazine* section featuring TEENFORM merchandise made with Celanese fabric. How do you think the timing of that ad will affect your sales potential? Naturally, our advertising program directed to the young girl and her mother continues in the consumer magazines such as *Seventeen, American Girl, McCall's,* etc. More about this next time!

Good luck!

Florence Scharf
Marketing Executive

SUGGESTIONS

(*see also* Ideas; Persuasions; *and* Proposals)

This category is for the minor brainstorm. You think it wise, helpful, desirable, for someone to take a particular action. You think you have a solution to someone else's problem, or one you share. Since the tone of the message is usually tentative—whether or not it's a good idea is not intrinsic but based rather on the recipient's reaction—keep these memos brief, uncomplicated, and to the point. If there's more to be said, let it be done in conversation. Consider the written message a communications starter.

A production executive nudges one of his subordinates to send a message to the head of another department expressing thanks for cooperation.

That was a great feat, getting the Ford job out on schedule. I understand that Bill Weebe of Expediting provided major help. A thank-you note from you to Bill might be in order. Yes?

"How about getting the treasurer to talk business to us."

Boss, I understand our Treasurer, Mr. Allen, gave a talk to the Research and Development people on the economics of our business. Don't you agree that production supervisors could benefit from some of the same? I've talked to some of the other department heads, and I'd say the reaction was favorable.

Can we discuss this briefly at our next meeting?

A contest on conservation.

We're all sold on the idea of cutting down on waste, conserving resources, etc. How about a prize contest, either for individuals, or on a departmental basis, to see who can come up with the best ideas?

A manager favors a departmental safety program.

I think safety posters give people a false sense that they're doing something about the problem by hanging up a piece of paper. I'd like to start a little formal program in my department. Could I meet with you to explain what I have in mind?

"If you're afraid to hit the streets alone at night . . ."

A suggestion for employees who work on the second shift: If you'd rather not walk to a bus or subway stop alone, let me know and I'll arrange to have you escorted by a guard or other employees going to the same destination.

A warehouse foreman suggests a solution to a late-delivery problem.

The other day you asked me what could be done to get material deliveries to your department at the start of the shift. How would it be if I bring in two men to start here at 8:30? But what I'd expect at your end is a couple of your people to help them unload promptly at 9:00. Think it would work?

THANKS

See Acknowledgments *and* Gratitude

VIEWING WITH ALARM

It's been said that politicians have two traditional stances: they point with pride, and on the other hand, they view with alarm. On the business scene, this latter type of message plays a constructive function. It can warn a subordinate of a deteriorating situation that would benefit from some specific attention; or it can voice to one's superior concern for a situation that is getting out of hand. When this message addresses itself realistically to a situation, the writer looks good because he has shown alertness, a sense of responsibility, etc.

Two hazards to avoid in this genre: crying wolf and exaggeration of the condition pointed out.

An executive communicates his concern about an impending decision deadline to an aide. Movie history tells us that all of these candidates lost out to Vivien Leigh.

To Mr. O'Shea

New York
November 21, 1938
CONFIDENTIAL

Dear Danny:

In connection with Scarlett: we're getting so close to the starting date of the picture that I'm commencing to grow fearful of losing any of our really good possibilities and I think we should make clear to Katharine Hepburn, Jean Arthur, Joan Bennett, and Loretta Young that they are in the small company of final candidates; and on my return I hope you will be able to tell me immediately the situation in relation to each of these.

I think the final choice must be out of this list plus Goddard and our new girl [Doris Jordan], plus any last-minute new-girl possibility that may come along.

DOS
Memo From David O. Selznick

A division manager writes of his dismay over a performance difficulty to a production foreman. The intention here is to get the foreman to start remedial action.

Can anything be done to cut the scrap and reject percentages on the semiautomatic lathes? Each month for the past quarter I notice the figures inching upward. I can't tell whether it's the equipment, the operators, or some other factor. But if we can't turn things around, our costs will be shot to hell—and us along with them.

224

A supervisor writes to his boss. Wisely, the message is not addressed to the personnel department, where the problem originates, but to the writer's superior, who packs more clout in dealing with personnel than would the writer.

I have just received a memo from the Personnel Department listing vacation days due the members of my department.

It is my contention that in almost every case, people have been deprived of one entire year of earned vacation. I cannot overemphasize the importance of getting this matter finally straightened out. In just one case—Bill Harmon's—should he terminate or resign, a couple of thousand dollars of compensation is involved!

We kind of ducked this issue last year. But credibility of the company is becoming involved. We announce that personnel get three weeks vacation after five years. Now it turns out that personnel don't actually *get it* until after *six* years. Some are beginning to wonder (halo effect) if the pension and retirement plan will also contain some unhappy surprises.

I address this memo to you in the hope that you will use your influence to get this matter clarified once and for all.

A manager writes to a personnel director, whose responsibilities include plant security.

Perhaps you're not aware of it, but recently some local kids have been using our parking lot for a drag strip after hours. Last night, a stock clerk, leaving late, was almost struck down by a hot-rodder. Would it be possible to have our security department set up some kind of procedure to eliminate this danger? Or possibly contact should be made with the local police. One way or another, we have to take some action to end this situation.

WELCOME   (*see also* Orientation)

People like to be greeted. Whenever we enter a place—even if we've been there many times but especially when it's unfamiliar—there is much reassurance in words of welcome. Basically, these signal the message, Here's a friend, or a well-wisher.

Under the Orientation heading you will find examples of welcome to a newcomer into an organization. However, the memos here concern other situations in which a warm hello raise the spirits of the greeted and enhance the image of the greeter.

Typically, an informal greeting is best given orally. But this message explains how it sometimes becomes appropriate to put it in writing. This memo was written by one department head to another, but a welcome-back-to-a-job-after-an-illness message is a gracious gesture suitable either up or down the line.

Passed your office this morning, and saw you surrounded by a large number of your friends obviously delighted to see you back. Instead of joining the long line, I thought I'd just use this means to let you know how pleased I am that you have recovered from your illness. Just that brief glimpse suggests that you are back to normal, which is fine to see.

I think it's only fitting and proper that we celebrate your return by having lunch together soon. I know you will be tied up for the next few days, but I will call you next week to set up a date.

Here is a message of welcome that does two things: In addition to a warm assurance that the new member will be cordially greeted, the writer also takes the occasion to build the image of the organization and makes the newcomer glad that he has joined.

As acting head of the Management Club, I want to welcome you to membership. Although participation is voluntary, we are proud of the fact that 85% of those eligible have joined. As a charter member I can tell you that in the three years of the organization's activity, it has been a source of stimulation, education, and good fellowship.

Fellow members join me in expressing their pleasure at your being with us. We hope you will have every cause to be happy over your decision.

The recipient of this memo left the company to take another job, then reversed the move and was given his former position. People who make this kind of excursion tend to be uneasy on their return—not being sure of their reception. A welcome memo in this situation will be well received, particularly when it can include, as this memo does,

After our meeting today, I got the impression that you feel awkward being back in the organization and regret ever leaving.

I think you're wrong. You were wise to take that job. I think that you would always have regretted not making the jump if you hadn't done so. Of course, I also think coming back was a good move. Your status here has not suffered. Of course, there is bound to be a little discomfort.

assurance that no permanent damage has been done.

You'll always find numbskulls around who think in terms of "loyalty to the organization." But these are also the very people who envied your getting that job offer. The fact that it didn't pan out is just one of those things. And, believe me, the little discomfort you may feel at first will soon be gone.

You may be interested to know that two other people on the executive staff—now up near the top—went through exactly the same experience that you did. Obviously, it has done their careers no harm. So, welcome back to the club. I, personally, am glad to see that homely face of yours around again. I'm sure there will be mutual benefits for all concerned.

Even bosses like to be told that someone is happy to have them back at work. This message by a subordinate reflects an obviously good personal relationship in which the writer feels he can speak freely and openly.

Cheers and hurrahs! The month you were away seemed to have seven or eight weeks in it. As everyone knows, there's no perfect boss. But with all your faults, it's good to have you back.

"YOU WERE RIGHT"   (*see also* Apology *and* "I Was Wrong")

A companion to the "I Was Wrong" message, it gives the writer a chance to make gracious acknowledgment of the recipient's shrewdness in a matter. In the history of recorded time no one has ever been known to react adversely to this message. This type of memo can be sent off with a glad heart because it surely will be well received.

An executive lauds the accuracy of a customer-relations manager's prediction.

With this morning's mail we passed the 500-mark in responses from our customers. Remember, *I* said we'd only get a dribble of response to our questionnaire. *You* said we'd go over 300. Let me be the first to rush forward and award you a Solomon (the brainy set's version of an Oscar) as wise man of the week.

One manager compliments another for his acumen in spotting the untenability of an employee-job match.

Beverly Greene just phoned in to say she was quitting. I know you told Tom Pauder this was going to happen. As you said, I guess she just felt she was underplaced in her job and didn't see any likelihood of getting out of the secretarial ranks in the near future. I guess if Tom had listened to you he could have saved himself a lot of unnecessary effort trying to make an impossible situation work out.

Proving that someone can be wrong, and still be right.

The news has just come through that we're going along with Dale Lewis's idea on the development of new sales territories. Even though your plan lost out, I thought it had a lot to recommend it and I admire you for sticking to your guns. If there is such a thing as defeat with honor, this is an example. I think you come off looking awfully good.

"You were right, but. . . ." A senior salesman writes to a young friend and colleague who's just struck it rich.

I don't want to be the skeleton at the feast, Bob. Few things are sweeter than applause, and there's not the slightest doubt that you deserve all the praise you're getting for landing the Schiffers account. You worked hard, put in long hours to get that juicy contract.

Just remember two things: the very fact of your time investment suggests that you had to pay a price for the success. Perhaps the same amount of energy spread over smaller firms might have brought you an equal, though less spectacular, result.

Secondly, you've now created a new set of expectations with your boss, and yes, with yourself.

Really, what I'm saying is that you've put yourself in a new ball game. The fans are likely to be pretty tough—unless you keep them happy.

228

"You seem to be right, but perhaps there's a mitigating circumstance."

You seem to have hit it right on the nose. I've just got a batch of layouts from the Art Department and they're just blah. If this is a sample of the new art director's ability—you said you felt he was weak in the creative imagination area—then we're in a bad way for fresh visuals.

Next time we get together, please tell me what it was about him or his work that led you to your conclusion.

However, a final thought: Let's not forget he's new in the job. And maybe it's unfair to expect him to deliver the goods first crack.

Persuaded by my own words of caution, I'm going to withhold judgment until there's more to go on.

The End? Of course not!

We hope it's a new beginning.

index